MW00811103

(especially) the Psalms. His approach is solidly within the tradition of magisterial Protestantism, untainted by fideism. He successfully brings out the strong philosophical arguments about God contained in the text—its implicit natural theology.

The book will appeal to both a popular and a more scholarly audience. Many Christians, puzzled by the book of Job and by the available commentaries on it, will find Anderson's book helpful and illuminating. Scholars will have to take Anderson's arguments into account, whether or not they find them ultimately convincing. I enthusiastically endorse the publication of the book.

Robert C. Koons is Professor of Philosophy at the University of Texas at Austin

Rarely does an insightful philosopher write a philosophical commentary on a difficult book in the Bible. Yes, many biblical scholars, theologians, and pastors have written about The Book of Job, but few, to my knowledge, have approached it as Owen Anderson has done. He considers moral evil in light of natural evil, the clarity of God's revelation, and God's purposes in suffering. It ends up that by being philosophical, he is also biblical, theological, and pastoral.

Douglas R. Groothuis is Professor of Philosophy at Denver Seminary

In his treatment of Job, Anderson moves beyond the familiar question of why bad things happen to good people to the even more fundamental question of whether life has meaning at all, inviting the reader into conversation with not only Job and himself, but also with other

great characters of world literature and even the divine. I found this manuscript to be of great interest and believe it will be engaging and valuable to readers from many different walks of life. I eagerly await the published book!

Jason Jewell is Director of the Center for Great Books & Human Flourishing at Faulkner University

Job is a daunting book to read, for obvious reasons. It is existentially troubling to confront the reality of God's sovereignty over everything, including suffering and evil. The church has been helped by scholars who have applied biblical and theological learning to Job, for which we should be thankful. Yet, as wisdom literature, Job deserves more than this kind of analysis. Owen Anderson's careful philosophical reading adds a depth not often encountered in commentaries, especially as he helps us deal with the very human search for meaning in the light of suffering. Anderson reminds us that this meaning is found in God, but is seen most clearly when everything in life is stripped away. By God's grace you will benefit from reading Job, and you will also benefit from reading this commentary. From both the Spirit will equip to glorify Job's Redeemer who lives, even in the midst of your own personal suffering.

Ian Hugh Clary is Assistant Professor of Historical Theology at Colorado Christian University

Foreword

Any book is the product of numerous influences and support. I have been studying and teaching philosophy for 25 years. During that same time, I have grown in my understanding of historic Christianity. Through my own struggles and trials, I have had the firsthand encounter with the problem of sin and suffering. The lesson of Job and the need for deeper repentance have been a reminder to me as I reflect on my own experience. In this same way, Job is a book for all of us.

My hope for this book is that it will bring the many philosophical lessons of Job into greater focus and by doing that help make the way straight for the Gospel. When Paul visited Athens, he encountered the philosophers gathered to talk about the latest ideas. Nothing has changed for philosophers. And yet the latest ideas are the same old ideas. Job anticipated solutions to the problem of evil counted as new and novel in our day. If philosophers understand basic things about God and the good, they will no longer be distracted by what counts as the latest ideas. Philosophy as the study of what is clear about God from general revelation can provide an account of knowledge of basic things.

I have many to thank for help on this project over the past few years. These include my parents, my pastor, my friends, and my wife. It has been a special part of this project to work with Alyssa to bring it to print.

Quotes from the Bible are from the KJV and NIV and at times I use the Book of Psalm for Singing when quoting the Psalms.

Table of Contents

Job Part One

The Prologue

3:25

For the thing which I greatly feared is come upon me, and that which I was afraid of is come unto me.

The problem of evil is a universal problem. All humans face it. It presses us to ask "why." It is not primarily a practical problem. The removal of suffering is not sufficient; we want to make sense of why there is suffering. This is why the problem of evil is a human problem: it is a problem of understanding.

The problem of evil requires us to more carefully define good and evil. What is this "evil" that gives us this problem? It is not enough to say that evil is what hurts someone because this does not explain what it means to hurt or do evil (these are synonymous). We must define these in order to know what is hurtful and what is beneficial. If we are to make progress, we need a definition of the good.

The problem of evil presupposes that the good is knowable. It is not sufficient to say that for all we know there is some greater good—one could also say that for all we know there is not some greater good. And if the good is not knowable then we do not know that there is a problem with "evil." Instead, the problem is precisely that we can and should know what is good, and we can and should know what is evil, and we want to make sense of suffering so that we can understand.

And this means that not only is the good knowable, but what is good is also clear. To say it is clear is to say we must shut our eyes to avoid seeing it. This is the heart of the problem of evil and what will end up making the problem ironic. The very person protesting about the problem of evil has shut his eyes to what is good. And this means that the solution to the problem is not just gaining greater information—as if the solution is a matter of coming to know some interesting or perhaps secret things. It also involves the need for repentance. The failure to know what is clear is culpable and without excuse. We should expect that the height of the story of Job will involve repentance and sanctification.

The book of Job is about meaning. What is the meaning of life? And what is the meaning of suffering? We are going to treat this book as a dialogue that requires us to also enter in and make the content our own. Meaning is a universal problem, which makes it all the more striking that the book of Job is given at this early point in human history: Job wrestles with a problem that has touched everyone. Before we come to redemptive revelation, we need to have understood moral evil and natural evil.

Why is there suffering? What is the meaning of it? How do we make sense of it? This is a universal and ancient question. "How do we make sense of suffering" is the question that presses us to ask about the purpose of moral and natural evil in the world. An answer to this question is what brings us to redemptive revelation. So it is not surprising that, at the beginning of redemptive history, we would get this early story of Job, which discusses how to understand suffering, sin, and our need for redemption. We can categorize the various world systems and world religions in terms of how they have answered these questions. The peoples of the world look for their comfort and safety in various solutions. In Job we get wrestling with God: not a god or a deity that is finite and limited, but wrestling with God the Creator. Job wrestles with the problem of meaning, of making sense of the world—he does not merely want to get out of suffering.

Fixed Points

There are some fixed points in the text for which any treatment of Job needs to account. The first is that right away, in chapter 3, Job asks a series of questions. These are "why" questions. Why did I not die from the womb (3:11)? They are about the meaning of life and of suffering. How a reader answers these questions (some common answers are: because God is sovereign and we cannot comprehend) will shape how that reader understands the book of Job.

If that is the first fixed point the last fixed point is that Job repents (42:6). We respect when we believe we have done something wrong. Therefore, Job thought he had done something wrong. And for something to have been wrong we must have been able to know it was wrong. If Job cannot have known it was wrong then he does not need to repent he just needs to be instructed. Job's repentance involves having been wrong and having failed to known what he should have.

If we combine these two fixed points we begin to see that they are connected and the material between them makes that connection. The answer to the "why" question involves knowing something about God's revelation that Job did not know but should have known. Is this unique to Job or is it universal?

There are other fixed points and there are also other interpretive contexts coming from general revelation. Together these then allow us to draw good and necessary consequences from the text to understand its meaning. Without these we will not draw these inferences and will not understand the meaning and will not only miss it but will obscure it even more with a misinterpretation that prevents ourselves from understanding and hinders others.

Some of these include Job offering atoning sacrifices at the beginning and end, God accusing Job of wrongdoing, God asking Job questions that need to be answered, God's questions are about the natural created world, Elihu not being reprimanded, that all of this account is what it took to get Job to see God, that the suffering (natural evil) was not a punishment, that moral evil requires a knowable standard. We will look at even more from the context of general revelation.

The Theodicy

A theodicy is an attempt to justify God's ways to man. As such the believer might reject the very idea because God's ways are above man's ways. The Book of Job is sometimes read this way as God declaring in the final chapters that He does not need to explain His actions because he is sovereign.

This is an insufficient theodicy and an insufficient reading of the Book of Job. The problem of theodicy is not to justify God's ways but to find meaning. How can we make sense of the supposed existence and nature of God in light of suffering and evil? Are these proofs that there is no God? We cannot simply begin by asserting there is a God and that God does not need to justify His ways because He is sovereign. This is the point at hand. This is what is questioned. We are asking for knowledge and meaning. Perhaps the whole idea of God is incoherent and we need to look elsewhere for meaning. The believer who says it is wrong to even entertain such an idea is in the place of a fideistic; any belief system can be asserted fideistically why should we accept this form of fideism over another? This is precisely the point Job is being pressed on from the beginning of the story.

To say that we are pursuing meaning is not the same as a greater good or soul making solutions. It may have some resemblance. But the essence of these is different. The soul making theodicy says that we need suffering to learn virtues like patience or courage. But virtues are not the same as the good. Virtues are a means to the good. And we only need patience and courage because there is suffering to deal with. So, to say we need suffering to learn patience so we can be patient in suffering hasn't given us an answer. It hasn't identified what the good is at which virtues aim.

The greater good solution says that God permits evil for some greater good. Formally speaking this is a true statement. But it all revolves around how that greater good is defined. If a philosopher says "for all we know there is a greater good" this is not a solution. For all we know there is not. What is the greater good? Or, what is THE good? Our chief end, highest value, that at which all things aim. What is it? Only when we have identified it can we then begin to make sense of suffering. Not only does suffering not threaten the good, it depends the good.

To state very clearly here at the beginning: our chief end is to glorify God in all that by which He makes Himself known, in all His works of creation and providence. It is to know God. And we know God from the works of God. The works of God display the glory of God. And so we have the problem of the Book of Job: But does not suffering offer a proof that the works of God are out of order. They are not well managed? God is distant or unconcerned? How can we make sense of suffering in light of God's existence and nature? And will suffering make us reject belief in God? Our goal here is to find meaning and make sense of it so that we understand and in doing this we have grown in our knowledge of God and His works.

The Commentaries

A survey of commentaries on Job will show that there are really only so many ways in which the book is approached. What new commentaries add is often simply more detailed descriptions from recent archaeological discoveries and comparisons with Canaanite mythology. What about the Babylonian Job? The Babylonian theodicy has a "Job" figure that reconciles himself to fideistic rule following the absence of knowledge. Additionally, word studies are done about Job, especially digging into understanding the poetry and the symbolism in light of its context at that time and what the different words mean. Many times the new commentaries are only about updating us on new discoveries of the meaning of the words.

There are standard answers about Job: that ultimately the solution in Job is a reiteration of the mystery of God, the unknowability of God. Or perhaps the displacement of man from the center; putting Job in his place. Or the book is a display of the power of God in response to Job's questions. Then there are some, like Maimonides, that say Job is a fictional dialogue written to display various answers given to the problem of suffering. One can look at the hero series and the quest of the hero and Joseph Campbell, and think of Job as that hero. We'll later look at that idea of Job as the hero. I would challenge anyone to think of a hero who goes through a greater trial.

There are many ways in which Job has been approached. We can think about these different methods and what each of them says about the persons who present them. In each commentator's case, we really learn more about the person and what they think of God when they give this interpretation of the book of Job. We must be conscious of how we are approaching the book.

I go through all these different commentators and views of Job to say that this book is not a standard commentary on the book of Job. It is a philosophical commentary. I will not do a search for the historical Job here—but nor will I dismiss the historicity of Job and instead make the story into an allegory. The problem that Job faces is both particular and universal. It is particular to each person and their circumstances. It is universal in that all persons face it. We are taking that problem as real and as basic. Other problems are oriented and fitted together in reference to that problem.

What assumptions are brought to an exegetical study? It is not simply enough to say that we are doing a word study. Words have meaning. In order to know their meaning, we have to know the context in which they operate. And this is not just the context of a sentence or paragraph. Or the way that same word is used in other settings. It is the context of what is real. This includes what is clear to reason from general revelation. Job had access to general revelation. We have access to that same general revelation. What can and should be known from general revelation? If a commentator approaches Job without knowing what is clear from general revelation then the commentary that is produced won't be able to find the meaning in the text that reflects general revelation even though it is right there the whole time. A fideistic or skeptical commentator who has neglected general revelation will produce a fideistic or skeptical commentary that neglects general revelation.

Job and Culture

The book of Job has worked itself into culture in a way that even those who have never heard of it, which may be increasing, can recognize quotes from Job. There may have been a time when everyone heard of Job, and increasingly it might be the case that people do not even know the books of the Bible, but they still know or recognize sayings from the book of Job. They might even use them and not know where they came from. "The Lord gives and the Lord takes away; blessed be the name of the Lord." Or, "Man that is born of a woman has but a short time to live and is full of misery." Or, "I know that my redeemer liveth, and that he shall stand in the latter days upon the earth." Thomas Carlyle said this about Job: "I call it, apart from all theories about it, one of the greatest things ever written with pen. One feels indeed as if it were not Hebrew. Such a noble universality, different from noble patriotism or noble sectarianism, reigns in it. A noble book. All men's book. It is our first, oldest statement of the never-ending problem of man's destiny and God's way with him here in this earth, and all in such free-flowing outlines, grand in its sincerity, in its simplicity, in its epic melody, and repose or reconcilement. Sublime sorrow. Sublime reconciliation. Oldest choral music as of the heart of mankind. So soft and great as a summer midnight, as the world with its seas and stars."

Job states for us a problem we all must address. The answers that are considered in the book of Job to the question "why do I suffer?" are still the same in kind that we hear today. Those answers have the same weaknesses. And those who cannot see the answer given in the book of Job also do not see the answer given in general revelation. We can see a refinement of the problem of evil in Job, even though it is dealt with everywhere.

The Universality of Job

The book of Job has universal appeal because it has universal content. It touches each of us in a way that is personal. We can relate to Job. There may be some things at first that put him at a distance from us: he is blameless. We may say, "this is not me, nor do I experience the kind and the depth of suffering that he goes through." In this book, I am going to try to make Job come alive and show that this book is the statement of man's problem.

If we have not dealt with sin and death, which is found in Genesis 1-3, we should not expect to find the answer that is in Job. It will elude us. And we see it does elude some otherwise astute thinkers. This is because the book of Job assumes the reader has basic things in place about the nature of God and man and good and evil, from general revelation. It also assumes the reader knows the Biblical Worldview of creation, fall, and redemption. With those in place, Job addresses the most pressing existential question we all face.

What is the answer here? Why do people get Job wrong so often and miss what happens in this book? What we are going to do is learn to think about this in light of seven layers of context. This context is necessary to learn how to interpret or understand. In other words, we begin with what is basic first. And we are not doing this merely as a kind of information session about Job, although I do hope my readers' information about Job increases. Rather, we are going through context because we are called to wrestle with this existential problem along with Job. And I think that is why we'll get to the universality of the book of Job—because we will find out that each of us has wrestled with this problem.

The Context of Job

Job's context includes general revelation. If a reader has themselves minimized or ignored general revelation then they will read Job in this same way. This is true if it is a believer or an unbeliever. There are things we should know as we approach the book of Job in order to understand the text. For instance, if we cannot read then we cannot understand Job. If we cannot make logical inferences then we cannot understand Job. But we can add that if we have not seen that there is a clear general revelation of the eternal power and divine nature of God then we will not understand Job. This means we should be able to show that only God has existed from eternity. The created order, including the material world and the human soul, have not exited from eternity. It includes the attributes of God including God's power, knowledge, and goodness. Additionally, that God is known through the works of creation and providence. As well that moral evil is the failure to seek, to understand, and to do what is right. Similarly, that natural evil is not a punishment but is imposed as a call back from moral evil. And that our highest good is in knowing God in all that by which He makes himself known (in all His works of creation and providence). These are knowable by all from general revelation. If a person does not know these things and reads this philosophical commentary then it is likely they will say that these were read into Job and are not present in the text. But the reverse is true. They are present as the context and by good and necessary consequence are seen throughout. The person who does not know about general revelation is guilty of not seeking and so will resist the message of Job and instead find a solution that justifies their not seeking (the answer is that there is no answer, or some such thing).

If we are older and we have gone through the trials of life, how have we understood them? How have we found meaning in our life? Do we mostly brush aside the trials and not think about them? We have also wondered about how to make sense of our lives and our suffering in the way the world is ordered. How is the world ordered? Is it ordered aright? If we were a visitor to this world and were told that it had been designed by a perfectly good and powerful God, would we believe it? What is the meaning of evil? That is going to be our central question.

Perhaps because people miss that question in their own life, they might miss it when they come to Job, and not make it the central question—they make another theme the central theme, like God displaying his power. They already miss the meaning of general revelation in their lives, so they don't see it in Job either. But with Job we want to ask, what is the meaning of this trial? What is the purpose of it? We must wrestle with that. There is universality to Job. We want to know why. How can we make sense of trials in life? Does life have any meaning? If there is no meaning, it would have been better to not exist. We'll go over those questions and we'll look at some of the answers given by Job's friends, his comforters.

The first part of Job is the Prologue, and it is a prologue to an argument. The body of the book is an argument: three arguments, three sets. The first part of Job is a prologue in the sense of setting up his argument, but we must also do a prologue that asks: what should we know as we come to the book of Job? A prologue is a "pre-word." What word do we already know before we come to this? I have already spoken of Job as part of the wisdom literature. Sometimes there is a tension said to exist within the wisdom literature between, for example, Job and Proverbs. Some say the Book of Proverbs presents a very simple view of life, where Job and Ecclesiastes are more nuanced and real. Proverbs says that the righteous prosper and the wicked are punished. Some of the things that Job's friends say to him sound like they are from Proverbs.

Job's friends, Job's comforters, push the message of the righteous prospering and the wicked suffering. But that is not what the Book of Proverbs is doing. It does affirm general truths about the connection between righteousness and the blessed life, but we also see in Proverbs the reality of that connection: the reality of wickedness and specifically how the wicked try to prosper in this life. The book of Job does not set aside the connection between righteousness and blessedness. It raises questions about just what those are and how we understand the storms of life. What do we think about—what do we already know when we come to the Book of Job? What should Maimonides have known when he came to the Book of Job? Or a current commentator?

We already had Genesis 1-3 in place. We should already know what Genesis 1-3 talks about the biblical worldview of creation, fall and redemption. Job is not before Genesis. This includes the clarity of general revelation, the divine power of God: the eternal power and divine nature of God, seen in Genesis 1:1. In the beginning God created the heavens and the earth. This means that there was a beginning. Something is eternal, God, and some things are not eternal, the creation. This is knowable from general revelation and is the opening line of special revelation. Special revelation begins this way to connect with what you should already know as you come to the text.

We should be able to show that only God, God the Creator, is eternal. We should be able to show the nature of God from the things that are made: God's eternal power and divine nature. We should be able to show that our highest good is in knowing God from the works of God, and this means that evil is the failure to know what is clear to reason about God. The consequence of sin, or moral evil, is spiritual death (rejection of reason means the loss of meaning). Natural evil (old age, sickness, death, toil, strife, famine, plague, war) is imposed on creation as a call back from sin. We have these as part of general revelation and the Biblical Worldview found in Genesis 1-3. If we don't have the biblical worldview in place then we won't understand Job. Or, what we do think about those topics will be demonstrated when we try to explain Job. Because Job is such a personal book, a person's attempts to explain what it means reveals much about that person.

We bring these beliefs about general revelation to Job. It includes creation as revelation: the works of God reveal God, so that should not be a surprise. If we already knew that coming into Job, many questions would be answered. The works of God reveal God. Creation ex nihilo is the foundation for the eternal power and divine nature. God made all things from nothing. Nothing is eternal along with God; God alone is eternal. The creation is very good. Now we are getting closer to Job. If we come to Job not knowing this about God, then we have not been seeking, and the content of Job is about us.

Something has happened so that evil, both moral and natural, has been introduced into the world. We ought to know this coming into the book of Job. As I was reading some commentators, I saw them stumbling on these points because they did not understand moral and natural evil ahead of time. They did not understand that creation is revelation, so they stumbled. Moral evil is a failure to live according to our nature: as autonomy; as not seeking, not understanding and not doing what is right. What's the purpose of moral evil? That is, why did God permit moral evil? Additionally, why did God impose natural evil? It is for the revelation of the glory of God. We see a deepening of the revelation of God's nature, especially the justice and mercy of God.

Natural evil is a callback from moral evil—it recalls from, restrains and removes moral evil. Thus, we already know the purpose of natural evil as we come into the Book of Job. The commentators struggled to make sense of Job on that point because they did not have those connections in place. Those who did not understand general revelation were the same ones who would say the point of Job is God's incomprehensibility: "We can't understand." I would guess they also struggle to make sense of God in their own life as they sort out the kinds of suffering that they are encountering, as well as the purpose of that suffering. Why is that suffering in their lives? We know already that natural evil is not a punishment. It serves some penal ends, but its purpose ultimately is to recall from evil. Natural evil might restrain moral evil, and it might teach some practical lessons, but ultimately its purpose is a callback from moral evil. We know that it is not merely educative, as in the soul-making theodicy view, which says that the purpose of natural evil is to make one into a better person. That view says suffering teaches us patience, and we need patience so that when suffering comes, we can get through it. See the circularity?

In addition to moral and natural evil, we also need to distinguish between root sin and fruit sin. When the Apostle Paul defines sin in Romans 3 (referencing David in the Psalms), he defines root sin: not seeking, not understanding, and not doing what is right. From general revelation the definition of root sin is not living according to our nature as a rational being. This is different from fruit sins that people often think of (theft, adultery, murder, etc.). Job's friends stumble on this point and an important part of the story is to find out what it takes to get someone to see their root sin. What will it take to get us to see our root sin and repent of it?

Natural evil calls us back from root sin, which is what we all share in common as sinners. Fruit sins may differ. We might have our favorite fruit sins to be horrified about when we look at others. We look at the publican and we are thankful that we are not him—yet we are like him. Job's friends wrestle with this point, and they are shocked at Job. It is intriguing to look at the progression in their discussions with Job. We are like the publican—we have gone astray. All, like sheep, have gone astray, which gets to our root sin. So just like Job himself will wrestle with getting that in focus, we should anticipate this as a kind of a-fortiori argument: we will wrestle with it. How hard will it be for us to wrestle with it? It was hard for Job. We will see what he went through: intense suffering over, say, a relatively short period of time—and what I mean is that it wasn't his whole life. For someone else who does not go through the intense suffering he did, it might take quite a bit longer.

Knowing God in All That by Which He Makes Himself Known

As we come to the book of Job, we know that our highest good, our chief end, or eternal life, is to know God in all that by which he is made himself known, in all his works of creation and providence. And we know we haven't done that. We have a problem. We need a covering through the death of another: vicarious atonement. Job affirms this as well and grows in it. And then, getting us closer to the problem of Job, we know of our need for integrity. Job worries for his own children; he is concerned that they might have cursed God. Job is told to curse God and die. And it is said of him, "In all this, Job did not give up his integrity." In these passages of Job (2:9-10, 27:5), this is a central concept: our need for integrity. Why is that important? If someone were to brush off integrity, then they would not be able to relate to Job. He is worried about his integrity. He wants a mediator to argue for him about his integrity. But how does this shape the interpretation of the Book of Job?

These things that we come to the book knowing—if we don't have those in place, we won't hear the message of Job. Others have come to this book without the doctrine of creation as revelation, and they stumble on it. The most common one I hear is that God just puts Job in his place. Job started to ask questions that can't be answered, and God flexes his muscles, and Job is quiet. It is mostly about humility. But notice: the humility is in the face of skepticism, which says it is presumptuous or prideful to expect knowledge and meaning. They say Job should embrace skepticism and be humble, because there is a sense in which the book is about pride and humility. But it is the humility in that we should have known these things and we did not. These things are knowable, and in our pride we defend ourselves. Job's friends get angry when he does not give in right away. Their pride flares up. They are furious. And each of them expresses themselves differently—they each have a different personality and approach to rebuking Job: first comforting, then rebuking.

There is some truth in many commentators' idea of the emphasis on the "mystery of God" and our inability to understand the ways of God. God's ways are above our ways. But that saying comes in the context of saying God's ways are perfect and our ways are not. It is not in the context of saying we can't understand anything. The saying is that we can understand that God's ways are perfect and ours aren't. So, we can understand God's ways. It is not saying we can understand nothing. Or how about this: "Do not lean on your own understanding." That as well is true. Don't lean on your own understanding; lean on the law of God. This is in contrasting our ways—our understanding—with God's ways: which are presented to us not as a mystery, as unknowable, but as the biblical mysteries—things that are gradually revealed. And as they become revealed, they are understood. They are beyond us in the sense that they come to us in special revelation from God, but they are present to us as truths to be affirmed and grown in. So those who emphasize the message of the book of Job as God flexing his power to put Job in his place, to humble him because he thought there were answers and there are no answers: this is missing it because they've already missed general revelation and what could be known of God. This is why I said at the very beginning that a person's view of Job says a lot about themselves and their own approach to God and the knowledge of God. Many commentators came with the view that God is unknowable, and they imposed it on the book. They have failed to know God from general revelation and consequently they think Job has this same failure.

Consider how this same theme is found in the Psalms. This wrestling is not limited to the book of Job. We see it in Psalm 119:71: "It was very good for me that I was humbled low." I was prideful. I thought I knew when I did not know. The answer is not to say that therefore nothing can be known. That is a continuation of the same pride. Rather one should say: I did not know and I should have known. We'll see if we can come to utter the words that Job uttered. Psalm 119: "It was very good for me that I was humbled low." Romans 8:28: do you believe that all things work together for the good? The psalmist says that the humbling was "good for him."

Job and General Revelation

If we do not have general revelation in place, we won't understand Job. General revelation allows us to define moral evil, to understand the purpose of natural evil, and to think about our need for atonement through the death of another. This is a reminder of how we are to come to any book. We can use general revelation now in our own reading of Job, but also as we approach the other books of the Bible and think about how we are understanding them; how we are interpreting them when we read the Bible. Job, living before the law of Moses, knew of this and offered sacrifices. He knew of his need for atonement through the death of another. Much is summarized in just that description of Job offering a sacrifice. We see it at the beginning and at the end. Job offered sacrifices as the story begins and then as it ends. The need for vicarious atonement through the death of another in the place of the sinner. This bridges general revelation and redemptive revelation. It is because there is a clear general revelation that unbelief is without excuse. And it is in this context that redemption is offered and sacrifice for atonement understood.

Who Was Job?

All of this is by way of prologue to the Prologue. What do we bring to the Scriptures to help us understand Job? I don't want to say Job is "the greatest book." We read other books, but like gems, there are special books; each one has its own brilliance that we get to enjoy. And this one is a very dear and special book that addresses a problem that we call the existential problem. How is the problem set up?

In the land of Uz, a region east of the Jordan, lived a man whose name was Job. This man was blameless. Look at the list it goes through: blameless and upright. He feared God and shunned evil (1:1) The fear of the Lord. The beginning of wisdom. That is why the book of Job is wisdom literature. He feared God, and in connection with that, he shunned evil. That is part of maturity: being able to discern good and evil—and Job is able to do those things. The idea of being blameless and upright is not the same as "sinless." This is a key distinction to keep in mind in the book. He is not sinless, but he is blameless of any of the sort of outward sins that someone could bring against him—and his friends will try. Don't we need friends like that? And it mentions some of what Job has in this first passage: seven sons and three daughters and the sheep and camels and oxen and donkeys and servants. He was the greatest man among all the people of the East.

This is going to be a significant story; a significant fall. The greatest man is also a God-fearing man. Don't we like that when we see someone in authority? We like to say, "oh, and also he is a Christian. He is not only the CEO of a company I like, but he is also a Christian." Or maybe a political leader who is also a Christian. We will say Job is the greatest man and he is a God-fearer. There is a kind of intuition that makes sense—he is doing so well because he fears God. And it is already setting us up for the same thing that Satan is going to use.

Job has a concern about his children and their condition. He talks about them having these feasts in their homes that they invite their sisters to. "When a period of feasting had run its course, Job would send and have them purified. Early in the morning, he would sacrifice a burnt offering for each of them, thinking, 'Perhaps my children have sinned and cursed God in their hearts.' And that was Job's regular custom" (1:5). So he has a concern for his family also. He is operating as priest or mediator in offering these sacrifices. Because one might wonder, why aren't the kids doing that themselves? They are adults. But their father is doing that. This was Job's regular custom.

Where does he get this idea of a burnt sacrifice? We can begin to put together Job, his timeline and his reference, and his knowledge of Genesis 1-11. The book, in Jewish Tradition, is written by Moses during his time in the desert. So he knows about the need for a burnt sacrifice. That is important: it is not just a sacrifice—there might be other kinds of sacrifices—but specifically the burnt sacrifice: something to die in the place of the other. vicarious atonement. We see this from the beginning in Genesis 3 and the coats of skin.

The Larger Spiritual Battle

And then we get to this challenge: chapter 1:6-12. "One day, the angels, the sons of God, came to present themselves before the Lord, and Satan also came with them." This is the accuser. There are different names for Satan, and this one means the accuser. There now is a debate structure for the book. We might mostly think of the three rounds of debate with his friends. But there is also a debate between Satan and God, or an accusation made by Satan against Job to God, which pushes Job to understand his need for a mediator who will respond to the accuser. We want to see what we can make of that without going too far, but without going too little: what can we make of Job's understanding? Satan the accuser comes, and God asks him a question. We have already met Satan. We know how he was described in Genesis 3. It is interesting that what God does with him is something similar: God asks him a question like he did of Adam. "What have you been doing?" Last time we met Satan in the text in the Garden of Eden, what had he been doing there?

"Where have you come from?" God asks. "Wandering. Going to and fro throughout the earth, roaming the earth" (1:7). How's that for an answer? Satan hasn't been doing much with himself, apparently. What if he would have responded, "Well, I've been having dominion over the things you made in order to see your excellence. I felt really bad about what happened in Genesis, in the Garden." We see that he is roaming the earth, but not for good ends—for mischief. And it is immediately obvious in what happens next.

Look at how it all starts for Job. Did we think Satan started it? Oh, no. Here it begins. God says, "Have you considered my servant Job? There is no one like him on the earth. He is blameless and upright, a man who fears God and shuns evil" (1:8). That is a touching description by God—and in doing that, he alerts Satan to Job. Satan is not instigating this in the sense of picking on Job. God brings up Job, and he brings him up with these fine descriptions. God does not mention here any shortcomings of Job. But he asked Satan that question. "There is none like Job in all the earth" (1:8). And Satan challenges this. Satan, just like he could have said, "Oh, I was going throughout the world having dominion," could have said, "I've been really impressed with Job's fear of you and how he shuns evil." He does not do that, though. He challenges God.

We are exposed to Satan's understanding. As I was talking to a youngster recently, he asked me, why is Satan so stupid? I said no, we don't want to go that route at all. He is wily, but there is a foolishness about it that is exposed here. We could call it the self-referential absurdity of Satan. And he will be lost in this darkness forever. I saw a church sign once that I kind of liked. It said, "If Satan ever reminds you of your past, remind him of his future." That is kind of clever. We get this problem for Satan. He is missing basic things that are clear to reason. And here he is challenging God; he is challenging God about the perseverance of the saints. If Job is a saint, Satan won't be able to do anything to him. And if he is not a saint, Satan has already got him. You can economize on your time, Satan. But Satan does not understand this; he does not understand God and the knowledge of God.

In general, what we will find Satan doing is using the tools of rationality while undermining them. He wants to appear to be wise and he is not. And he wants to appear here to challenge God. God had this description of Job and Satan challenges it. "'Does Job fear God for nothing?' Satan replied. 'Have you not put a hedge around him and his household and everything he has? You have blessed the work of his hands so that his flocks and herds are spread throughout the land, but stretch out your hand and strike everything he has, and he will surely curse you to your face'"(v9-11). Satan claims that Job only loves God for what Job gets. Job's love is for sale. So, we get into the first level: take all that Job has, but don't lay a hand on his person. We don't want to pass over this point quickly. As mentioned earlier, the commentators' understanding is exposed and comes short when they speak about Job. Satan's understanding is on display for us. It was put on display by God asking him questions to get to know where he is at. Satan has come short and he is said this about Job—and this is the very thing that Job was worried about for his kids: that they'd curse God.

Satan says he will curse you—to your face even. It is one thing to curse when God's not around, but he says Job will curse you to your face when you take these things from him—he only loves you for that. God—the Lord—Yahweh—the one in redemptive relationship—says to Satan, "Very well then, everything he has is in your hands. But on the man himself, do not lay a finger." So Satan goes out, and we have that description of a day when his sons and daughters are feasting and drinking and a messenger comes to Job and says, "The oxen were plowing and the donkeys were grazing, and the Sabeans attacked and carried them off. They put all the servants to the sword and I am the only one who's escaped" (v14). We have repetition of this: another messenger is coming up about the sheep. This time, fire of God fell from the sky and burned up the sheep, and while he was still speaking—the rapidity of this! — while he is still speaking, another messenger comes up and says, "The Chaldeans formed three raiding parties and swept down on your camels and carried them off. They put the servants to the sword and I am the only one who has escaped" (v17). And even while he is still speaking, another messenger comes up and says, "Your sons and daughters were feasting and drinking at the oldest brother's house when suddenly a mighty wind swept in from the desert and struck the four corners of the house and it collapsed on them and they are dead, and I am the only one who's escaped to tell you" (v18-19). All that he has—the book began in chapter 1 with a description of everything he has—is so quickly taken from him.

Job's response is at the end of chapter 1, in verse 20. Job gets up and tears his clothes and shaves his head and he falls on the ground and worships. He says, "'Naked came I from my mother's womb, and naked I will depart. The Lord gave; the Lord has taken away. May the name of the Lord be praised.' And in all this Job did not sin by charging God with wrongdoing' (v20-22). Chapter 1: the integrity of Job. I don't know many that could have gone through that. Only Job. What kind of losses have we encountered? Why is God doing this to the most righteous person? But Job does not curse God.

The Second Test

Satan has once again been asked a question: "Where have you come from?" Wandering around, wandering the earth, looking back and forth in it, presumably to cause mischief. And so God asks the question again: "Have you considered my servant Job? There is no one like him. He is blameless and upright, a man who fears God and shuns evil, and he still maintains his integrity though you incited me against him to ruin him without any reason" (v3). Have you considered Job, when he is now gone through this? God puts this back on Satan.

Remember, Satan has just been proven wrong; did you catch that? Satan said, "If you take these things, he will curse you to your face." Job did not, and God points it out. Job still maintains his integrity, God says, though you've incited me against him, to ruin him without any reason. What does that mean, "without any reason"? That is on Satan. You did this, Satan. What is Satan's purpose in any of this? He presents himself as if he has a reason. "I am exposing that Job's love is for sale. Just so you know. You may not have known that about your servant Job." But Satan has been shown wrong. "Well," Satan says, "skin for skin. A man will give all he has for his own life, but stretch out your hand and strike his flesh and bones, and he will surely curse you to your face"(2:4). Why should anyone believe Satan at this point? He has already been shown wrong in his assessment of when people do and don't curse God. But he is doubling down again.

Now, I am not suggesting Satan can repent, but I am putting it out there in the sense that he has been asked a question, and there are other ways to respond to the question. He could have said, "Yeah, I was wrong about Job; I am really sorry. In our last conversation, I assessed him one way but I was wrong." That is a fine answer, isn't it? Instead, he doubles down. Skin for skin. So the Lord says, "'Very well then, he is in your hands, but you must spare his life.' Satan went out from the presence of the Lord and afflicted Job with painful sores from the soles of his feet to the top of his head. Then Job took a piece of broken pottery and scraped himself with it as he sat among the ashes" (2:6-8). This, I think, is the bottom. I mean, someone might find some other way to get to the bottom or describe the bottom. Sitting on a pile of ashes. Painful sores. I remember one time I got a sunburn on my back and was just in absolute agony for about 48 hours. Nothing would help. I can't really reach my back to scrape it with broken pieces of pottery. And I would think that is less than what Job is going through: head to toe in pain.

In verse 9, his wife comes to him. "Are you still holding onto your integrity? Curse God and die!" Who's left after your wife? "You are still holding on to your integrity?" The implication is, that is foolish. Just curse God and die. Let go. Interestingly, Job does not go that direction. He goes a different direction, which is the better direction, but he also wonders about staying alive, which I'll focus on shortly. Curse God and die. That is one of the themes in all this. Did Job's children curse

God? Satan says Job will curse God to his face. His wife says curse God and die. Cursing God: what does that mean? Have we heard of any commandments about that? Is that same commandment about integrity? Do not take the Lord's name in vain. That is how we curse God.

And what if God draws to our attention that we have taken his name in vain—not in the way we thought but in a different way, a more basic way? The integrity theme is all throughout the book. It is the answer to the book, and if we miss it in general revelation, we won't get the book. Job is tempted in this way by this other person, by his very wife, and he overcomes it. Chapter 1 ends by saying that in all this, Job did not sin by charging God with wrongdoing. "In all this, Job did not sin in what he said" (v10b).

Job's Friends

At the end of chapter 1, we get a description of his three friends, whom we'll get to know more later. Here we look at round one. (How many rounds does this match go?) In round one, we'll fill out the personalities or characters of the friends, because we can see quite a bit about them and how they approach Job's problem. We might have met an Eliphaz. We might be an Eliphaz. Or perhaps more of a Bildad. Or a Zophar. These men hear about Job's troubles—and these are wise men of the time. They are notable wise persons in their own right who come to help him understand his problem. They heard about his troubles, so they set out from their homes and meet together by agreement to go and sympathize with him and comfort him. What are Job's comforters bringing? Would anyone like comforters like this? William Blake had a drawing of Job's comforters. What will bring comfort? "Comfort ye my people." Redemption comforts, and that begins with confession of root sin. Job's friends don't get there; they need to repent.

When the three friends saw Job from a distance, they could hardly recognize their dear friend, and they "began to weep aloud and they tore their robes and sprinkled dust on their heads. They sat on the ground with him for seven days and seven nights, and no one said a word because they saw how great his suffering was" (12-13). Who has suffered like this man has suffered? Here we are introduced to these three friends and how they are going to try to comfort him. Their comfort is in the context of piety. Not one of them is an atheist or a platonic dualist. And because of that, their comfort is more subtle and we need to work our way through that. Each of them appeals to God and the righteousness of God. And part of what may have thrown them off when they saw their friend was precisely this: how can this happen to the righteous? It was not just what they saw for their own friend, but also how it threw their own understanding of the world into chaos. How could this have happened to Job? They will need to make sense of it.

Job and the Question of Meaning

But before that, in chapter 3, Job speaks. Whereas his wife had said, curse God and die, Job looks backwards, to his very existence. Because if we die, we are still there with the same problem: why did this happen? And Job's concern is to find meaning in it. If it is meaningless, it is not that we should die; it is that we should not have even existed. Existence should have meaning. He curses the day—not God—the day of his birth. "May the day of my birth perish, and the night it was said, 'A boy is born!' That day—may it turn into darkness. May God above not care about it. May no light shine upon it. May darkness and deep shadow claim it once more. May a cloud settle over it. May blackness overwhelm its light" (v3-5). We get here some introductory poetry of Job, as the book moves from more of the description of the contest into the poetry that Job and his three comforters display. Job wishes he would not have even lived. Life makes no sense. He does not want to exist. He is not cursing God, but he is connecting up the need for meaning with existing.

We can consider how Hamlet wrestles with that. He was puzzled about something similar; wondering how life could go so badly wrong that a man murders his brother to marry his wife. Hamlet says that the world is like an unweeded garden that grows to seed; things rank and gross in nature. But even Hamlet is just looking into the future, into dying, lamenting that the Everlasting has "fixed his cannon against self-slaughter." He finds nothing profitable in the world, he says. Job is going further than Hamlet I think, and doing a better job of raising the question about the very meaning of it all. If there is no meaning to it, I should not have even existed. It is not enough just to exist, realize there is no meaning, then kill yourself. What's the meaning of life?

We can think about it in contrast to Macbeth: that "tomorrow, creeps in this petty pace from day to day, to the last syllable of recorded time; All our yesterdays have lighted fools the way to dusty death. Out, out brief candle! Life's but a walking shadow, a poor player, that struts and frets his hour upon the stage, and then is heard no more. It is a tale told by an idiot, full of sound and fury, signifying nothing." Here we have the same wrestling: but unrepentant wrestling, ultimately cursing God. Life is a tale told by an idiot. For the tale in that case, the playwright, is God. So Macbeth does not preserve his integrity. But these are two examples of persons who see that problem.

Job is going back to his very beginning. If we exist, we expect meaning. And if there is no meaning, then why did we exist at all? What is God's purpose in this? Why did I not perish at birth and die as I came from the womb? Why were there knees to receive me and breasts that I might be nursed? For now, I would be lying down in peace; I would be asleep and at rest with kings and rulers of the earth, who build for themselves places now lying in ruins, with rulers who had gold, who filled their houses with silver. Or why was not I hidden away in the ground like a stillborn child, like an infant who never saw the light of day?" (3:11-16). All of this ends in the same thing. Hamlet actually does that as well in his discussion about Yorick, whose skull he is holding. And after he considers Yorick, he says, Yorick is now in the dust, but do you know who else is in the dust? Alexander and Caesar. That is the end of all of us. Why were you born if there is no meaning to it? All these kings who make these places for themselves (v19). Incidentally, given the timeframe of Job, we can think about someone like Gilgamesh or Nimrod, who think they will achieve immortality by building great cities to themselves. And now they lie in the dust.

Some people try to extrapolate from this something of Job's view of the afterlife, and that he did not believe in the afterlife. Later I'll make an argument that no—instead, Job's point is about what comes of life. People can make these great palaces for themselves. There are those who seem to live large and prosper. They are able to build great monuments for themselves with their wealth. They are able to achieve great things and are revered among humans. The works of their lives are meant to be remembered. And yet it all comes to nothing. A chasing after the wind. It all returns to the dust. Gone. It is lost in the end of life. Why even live if that is the case? The person ends up in the grave and their work does not change that ending.

So here in 3:20 we get the statement of the problem, which will carry us through the book from Job's perspective. We know the challenge from Satan and we know God's questioning of Satan, having proven Satan wrong once so far. Satan said Job would curse God to his face on that first round and Job did not. Now we are in the second round, and now we get the problem from Job's perspective.

"Why is light given to those in misery, and life to the bitter of soul, to those who long for death that does not come? Who search for it more than for hidden treasure, who are filled with gladness and rejoice when they reach the grave? Why is life given to a man whose way is hidden, whom God has hedged in? For sighing comes to me instead of food; my groans pour out like water" (3:24). Psalm 88 has that same kind of wrestling. But the only other person in scripture that wrestles in this depth, and says something exactly like this, besides the psalmist, is Jeremiah. Jeremiah 20:14-15. We know Jeremiah as well: he was blameless as a prophet even in the face of the suffering he went through.

Job then states the problem. Why? What is the meaning of it? That is what he wants to know. And the culmination of these chapters is in what Job says in 3:25: "What I have feared has come upon me; what I dreaded has happened to me. I have no peace, no quietness. I have no rest, but only turmoil." Do we ever say that? "What I greatly feared has happened to me." How are we going to make sense of that in light of it being said that Job feared God? What did Job truly fear? How is this going to press his understanding? What do we fear? What do we love? What would happen if what we greatly feared happened to us? How would we respond?

Think of the image of the man who builds his house on the sand and the storm that comes that way. Have we built in a way that we would be able to weather that storm? We might say, "Well, I built for a Category 1 hurricane, not a Category 4." Job is going through The Storm. "What I greatly feared has happened to me." And we are all going to benefit by reading that, as we all think to ourselves, Oh, I hope this does not happen to me. How would we do? And we certainly will have turmoils and trials of life, though I don't know that they will be at the level of Job because we are not blameless. We'll be fine. Don't worry. But we will certainly have trials.

Have we prepared ourselves for trials? Will we curse God and die? Or are we ready for those as well? What do we greatly fear? Why do we do what we do?

How do we act to gain what we want out of life? What are we trying to get? And how much do we do to prepare? How much of our life is spent in trying to avoid what we fear? Apart from fearing God, we fear losing these other things and we spend our life trying to protect those things. This is a universal problem that all humans must face individually. We must give an account.

Job's Friends

In Job's first three chapters, we are introduced to the characters and the problem. The characters include God and Satan, and will also include the three friends and their responses. These are very pious friends. They will be subtle in their claims in the sense that say many true things. They are going to appeal to God and to righteousness and then accuse Job. And I think we can say that adds to the pain of Job. These are his friends. With friends like that, who needs enemies? As Job was suffering, he was also mocked. Christ was also mocked: "You who have saved others, come down from there and save yourself." Job has that same pain here as he is accused in the midst of this by his friends. But Job also has a Friend. In the next chapters we will get into that.

There are important things we know as we come to this book and we must keep them in mind. These were mentioned already as the context of the book of Job. The extent to which we know these and keep them in focus will be the extent to which we are able to interpret and find meaning in this book. We know as we read through Job that our highest good is in knowing God. We know about the clarity of general revelation, and we know the biblical worldview in Genesis 1-3 and the reality of moral evil and natural evil. So we know about Satan and his role as accuser.

We have already met Satan and heard the question he asked last time, in the Garden. Last time it was, "Did God really say?" And this time it is a question about

Job's integrity. "Does Job really have integrity, or will he curse you to your face?" So we know that the accuser, the adversary, tempts in that way by raising questions about our understanding, and he comes short in his understanding of God and of Job, and we'll need to go further with Job in making sense of this. And if it does not make sense, why should I want to live?

As we get into the three rounds with Job and his comforters, there is anguish and pain. We can see that picture of Job sitting on the ash heap in physical pain. This is not like he is at the pub enjoying a conversation with his friends. His friends may be wrong, but is it even a nice setting? There is the anguish Job is in and the pain he is in while they are bringing these accusations.

We will ultimately see overcoming, and if we are prepared to read it, we will see repentance from root sin and a growth, in a sinner, unlike any presented to us. Job, in his blamelessness, will repent of that root sin. If we did not know about it coming into the book, we won't see it. We will miss it in Job and we will miss it in ourselves. But if we did know about that in coming to the book, we will be awestruck. That word "sublime" is appropriate when this divine forgiveness is carried out into Job's life. We need to understand the witness in the life of Job and be able to do that same thing in our own lives and make sense of Romans 8:28. We need to be able to find joy and meaning. We find joy through meaning that we have in life, even in what appears to say the world does not make sense. That very thing is what deepens the revelation of God to us. Job's Friend will call him to repent of root sin.

Job Part Two

The Patience of Job

7:20
If I have sinned, what have I done to you, you who see everything we do? Why have you made me your target? Have I become a burden to you?

Round 1

How do Job's comforters argue, and how does Job reply? This section is round 1. There are three comforters and three replies. This round gets into each of their understandings. It is also an application to ourselves. Where are we at in our understanding? Do we know God and how God works in redemptive history? Job's friends claim to know this. Job's friends are not atheists. Imagine Epicurus jumping out and saying, "There is no God." We don't find that here with the comforters because they profess to understand God and God's ways. We might find out that we are like Job's comforters. We might know persons like them, and we might even be like them.

What exactly is the problem that we are going to be looking at here, that Job poses for himself, and that his comforters don't get—they speak past it? Job wanted meaning. He wanted to make sense of his suffering and his life. Do we know the meaning that is in the world as God rules in history?

Job's Condition

We are reminded of Job's miserable condition. Remember how all this began? Some of the beginning parts Job does not know about, yet we are given a glimpse into it. God says, "Have you considered my servant Job? There is no one on earth like him; he is blameless and upright, a man who fears God and shuns evil." "Does Job fear God for nothing?" Satan replied. "Have you not put a hedge around him and his household and everything he has? You have blessed the work of his hands, so that his flocks and herds are spread throughout the land. But now stretch out your hand and strike everything he has, and he will surely curse you to your face" (1:9-11). And then begins Job's trial, and he is unaware of what happened. Satan has this desire to thwart the plans of God, but all of Satan's plans are later thwarted. There is a story here which shows one way of God being tried. "Have you considered MY servant Job?" God calls him that, and so Satan will put God and God's works to the test, and we should not be surprised by that in Satan.

Satan cannot perhaps change the status of a Christian before God, but he can work to make their lives miserable, to deplete them of their energy so they are not vital, not maintaining any vigor, not growing. A miserable Christian. And then when the world looks at these miserable Christians, do we think they will say, "I want to join that group"? That is another part of Satan's plans. Make Christianity unattractive. The Christians go about miserable—it is called the measles and mumps of the soul. When a Christian goes about miserable or superficial in their suffering, they may have the measles and mumps of the soul. They are not understanding and not finding meaning. Job is held up, by God, for us to consider. "Consider my servant Job." That is not just at the beginning; that is through this whole process. Consider how Job suffers.

The Patience of Job

Job's patience is commended in James 5:11. "Indeed, we count them blessed who endure. You have heard of Job's perseverance and have seen what the Lord finally brought about. The Lord is full of compassion and mercy." We have heard of the perseverance of Job, the patience of Job. That is a well-known saying from James. And when we see the end intended by the Lord, we see the Lord is very compassionate. James connects up those attributes of God. Those attributes of God, the glory of God, are displayed in the life of Job and the suffering of Job. There are parallels in the suffering of David, and both of them point us to the suffering of Christ. Isaiah 66:1-2 shows this glory of God that is displayed on us, this light—and are we seeing it? Have we ever really considered God's servant Job?

How To Interpret Job: Root and Fruit Sin

Job is held up for our consideration, and as we look at this first round of dialogue between Job and his comforters, a few principles must be kept in mind. These relate directly to what Job could have known and what we all should know when we enter into suffering, as they guide us in our understanding of the narrative of Job. So, the first principle is: we interpret Job in light of the biblical worldview. That should not be a surprise. God is known from general revelation. God is known from creation. And that creation is purposefully a revelation—God's providence is revelation. We are here the unfolding of God's providence in the life of Job. And knowing this, knowing God, is our highest good. Secondly, our attention needs to be on fruit and root sin and the distinction between them. Fruit and root sin: have we ever repented of our root sin? That should strike the fear of God into us. Then third: natural evil and its purposes. I don't see that paid attention to either as I read commentaries on Job. There are three purposes of natural evil: it restrains, recalls, and removes moral evil.

Suffering and Sin

In suffering, we take our eyes off ourselves and we put them on God. We consider the works of God in creation and province, and consider the reality of moral evil and its depths at the root. We remember the purpose of natural evil. We remember the example of Christ and his suffering.

How does this work out here in Job? We get to round one and look at these three persons. Did they understand the points I just covered? Did they understand that creation is revelation? Did they understand root and fruit distinctions? Natural evil and its purposes? Were these three persons, who speak very highly of God, vital themselves? Had they ever confessed their root sin? Had Bildad done that? Is that too much to ask? I'd like to know that. Do we get that conviction of root sin in these three? They profess belief in God. How many people profess belief in God? "I believed in God since I was born. I fell out of the womb believing in God. And then some time later, I came to accept Christ." Was there no root sin in this person's life? How do they understand themselves?

One could believe something without understanding it in some sense. Many people profess things that they don't understand. Sometimes we are even told that it is the right thing to do—profess it even if you don't understand it. Job's friends do not get to root sin in their conversion, in understanding themselves. They don't see themselves, perhaps, as root sinners. They overestimate their grasp on truth and do not consider their own assumptions or counterexamples, which we'll be doing with them. They misapplied the truth. They claimed to know. However, there are many times when they say true things. We might look at what they say and think, wow, these guys are on to something there—Eliphaz is quoted in the New Testament. But when we look at them in totality, they don't understand these things. And they go from a kind of gentleness with Job to stern rebukes. They lack the milk of human kindness that we'd expect in friends. It is somewhat startling. And that is displaying their own lack of understanding. So, it is no wonder when we come to the end that God charges them with folly and slander.

Job sufferings were brought on him because of the fact that he is blameless. "Consider my servant Job." The long duration and intensity of Job's suffering serves the purpose that God has in displaying his glory in his redemptive works. What does it take to get Job to see root sin? That is what we are going to be seeing in this book. This is what it takes. That is why I asked jokingly, "do we really want to learn? Do we want to be like Job?" Well, one might say, I'll read the Cliff Notes version of Job and learn that way. I won't even read Job. There is much suffering involved in Job.

Adding to his suffering—adding to Satan's striking of Job's body with physical affliction—are these "friends." I have said before and I'll say again: With friends like these, who needs enemies? Are these what we call "frenemies"? They are insufferably pious. And they come to instruct God's servant Job in their piety.

Eliphaz: The Righteous Do Not Suffer

Eliphaz begins in chapter 4. These are arguments; they give a conclusion and they give supporting points. We will analyze the arguments. This first one from Eliphaz has six parts. Of the three friends, Eliphaz is the most sophisticated and gentlemanly—at least in how he begins. They progress from the first round, to the second round, to the third round, and they all end up changing in their approach. Perhaps Eliphaz changes the most dramatically because he is the gentlest at first, and he is the most adept in dealing with ideas. He is comfortable wrestling through ideas. So, he responds in a measured way in his first series of arguments, and that changes when Job pushes back.

Do we know an Eliphaz? Someone who likes to talk about theology and ideas and may say true things about God? Yet they haven't considered root sin. It does not seem to touch their lives. Many people think like that; they view themselves as very smart and very academic. They can wrestle with ideas, and it is not real; it is what was called in the first great awakening a "vital piety." It is not vital. It is piety, but not a vital piety.

The overall argument for Eliphaz is that the innocent prosper. What is the implication? You are not prospering. Do the syllogism: you are not innocent. So, in the first part, Eliphaz tells Job it is his turn to be taught. This is Job 4:2-6. You have taught others, Job; now it is your turn to be taught. You should be patient and listen and learn. And in the second part, Eliphaz gives his formula. This is really the formula that guides all three of these speakers. Thirdly, he is going to tell us about his own religious experience that guides him, that shaped his thinking. And fourth, he goes over why it is foolish to question the formula he gave us.

Then Eliphaz gives his advice—he hands down his advice from on high. Was not that kind of him? Then he gives some platitudes about the blessed man and the blessed life. And a lot of this could be summarized as platitudes. Humans fall into platitudes. We empty terms of meaning and we speak in platitudes. And so, when these friends receive pushback, they don't know what to do. They just get upset; they argue. They don't actually think about Job's responses—and Job has some good responses for them.

Eliphaz begins by asking permission. "If someone ventures a word with you, will you be impatient?" What stands out about that question, given whom he is talking to? The patience of Job is commended in Holy Scripture itself. Will you be impatient? This is the person you *don't* ask that question to. But, in Eliphaz's mind, who can keep from speaking, in the sense of how wrong Job has been? He says (here's his formula in 4:7), "Consider now: who, being innocent, has ever perished?

Where were the upright ever destroyed?" They weren't. If you are good, you would not die. You are dying, therefore, do the math. Figure it out. Is that correct? But it is going to take 30 plus chapters to wrestle with that.

This is blameless Job with whom he is talking. As Eliphaz observed, "Those who plow evil and those who sow trouble reap it. At the breath of God, they are destroyed. In the blast of his anger, they perish. The lions may roar and growl, yet the teeth of the great lions are broken. The lion perishes for lack of prey, and the cubs of the lioness are scattered" (4:11). These three speakers constantly refer to and uphold the sovereignty of God and the goodness of God and the justice of God. Look at Job's condition: clearly, he is a sinner. What could be more obvious?

So there is Eliphaz's formula. There really does not need to be much more of the book. We could end the book of Job at 4:7. We'll have chapter 4 verse 8, Job repents, and we are done. Why do we keep going? Because this is why there is a dialogue. This is what a dialogue does, especially a question-and-answer dialogue. We are going to draw out that understanding. Do you understand what you've just said, Eliphaz? What does it mean to say Job is a sinner, that he is not innocent?

Eliphaz keeps going. Beginning in 4:12, there is something interesting about his personality—remember, he is most comfortable wrestling with ideas. Here he tells us he had a religious experience. "A word was secretly brought to me. My ears caught a whisper of it. Amid disquieting dreams in the night, when deep sleep falls on men fear and trembling seized me and made all my bones shake. A spirit glided past my face and the hair on my body stood on end. It stopped." A spirit was before my face. "Man of the worldly mind," it said. No, that was a Christmas Carol reference. "A form stood before my eyes and I heard a hushed voice: 'Can a mortal be more righteous than God? Can a man be more pure than his Maker? If God places no trust in his servants, if he charges his angels with error, how much more those who live in houses of clay, whose foundations are in the dust, who are crushed more readily than a moth? Between dawn and dusk, they are broken to pieces. Unnoticed, they perish forever. Are not the cords of their tent pulled up, so they die without wisdom?'" If there is a question about where the speaking of the spirit ends, I think it ends there.

What is the view of man being given here? It is curious—like being embodied makes you a sinner, and the spiritual angels are better than humans because of that reason. It is said in scripture that we are a little lower than the angels. But this has to get fleshed out in Eliphaz's thinking: what is he saying here? We don't have to just speculate; he brings out in his own words how he understood this spirit. But what's interesting is he just takes it as true. I am not questioning if he saw a spirit; that is another interesting discussion. But he heard something and he just takes it as true. Don't believe everything you hear. "But it appeared as an angel of light." All the more, don't believe it. Why would he think this is true? Yet it shapes his whole thinking. He gave us his formula in verse 7, and he gives us his religious experience starting in verse 12, and it shapes him throughout the rest of the discussion.

Now Eliphaz goes on to say it is foolish to question these things. "I myself have seen a fool taking root, but suddenly his house was cursed." This shows how he is gentle compared to Zophar, who said: "His children are far from safety, crushed in court without a defender." Eliphaz is talking abstractly; Job's children were just killed, and that happens when the children are not pious. So, in one way, he handles it gently compared to his friend, who's more direct—"your kids"—but it is still harsh. We know why this happened. Eliphaz also talks about the fool. We don't like the fool, he doesn't like the fool, so we are all on the same side. No—we need to get past words and get into the content and the meaning of what's going on. Then he gives us advice—he gives Job advice. "If I were you, I'd appeal to God. I would lay my cause before him." It is as if Eliphaz thinks this has not occured to Job.

Job says this many times: I wish I could lay my cause before God. But Eliphaz is not talking about that. He is talking about fruit sins here. We'll see later what he accuses Job of. And he goes on here and says great things about God. God performs wonders that cannot be fathomed; miracles can't be counted. He bestows rain on the earth. He sends water upon the countryside. In the three friends' dialogues and in Job's dialogue, they say things that anticipate what God says. So we have to consider, how is this different from what God says? What is God saying at the end, exactly, that is any different than what these guys say? Even Job says these things. God thwarts the plans of the crafty, so their hands achieve no success. He catches the wise in their craftiness.

Discipline

In the next section, natural evil serves mostly as a kind of correction. Those who are doing crafty things are corrected by natural evil. God gets them. And then Eliphaz says, "Blessed is the man whom God corrects, so don't despise the discipline of the Almighty" (5:17). Is that good advice? We are told the same thing in Hebrews, to not despise God's discipline. And that is why it is important to get past platitudes and empty sayings. Don't despise the discipline of Zeus—yet now we are talking about the discipline of God. Who is God? What is he disciplining you for? What does it mean to know God? Can we articulate what that is? Eliphaz describes this person: like a tree planted by water, you'll come to the grave full of vigor, with sheaves gathered in season. And look how he concludes: "We have examined this and it is true. So hear it and apply to yourself" (5:27). We have gone through these ideas about God and how it works out; they are true. Go and do likewise, Job. Apply it now. Eliphaz does not expect what happens next; that is why he gets a little bit thrown off guard. "It's foolish to question what I have just said. It's based on my religious experience and a well-known formula." That is a solid argument, isn't it? What else does Job have left? It would be foolish to argue against Eliphaz.

What do we say to an Eliphaz? Do we know an Eliphaz? Have we ever been one? Have we had a friend in need of comfort and we brought platitudes to him? "You've fallen on hard times, you are clearly a sinner. I knew you were a sinner. I knew this would happen to you. I was just waiting for it to happen, to be honest. Now that it has happened, I can let you know. You are a sinner. Well, I kept my distance, but my love of God forces me to come talk to someone such as you." What do we say to an Eliphaz? What does Job say? What do we say to ourselves if we have been an Eliphaz? Eliphaz is not operating out of the biblical worldview. He has a form of outward piety and sensibility; he appeals to our longing for security and ease; he puts his finger on the sense that we as humans are sinners. And we feel that—we are sinners. As I said before, he is not himself been convicted of sin and death; he is unable to witness to Job about this. The sins he refers to are fruit sins. He has not seen his own root sin.

What will it take for God to display that—to get a human in their argumentativeness, in their self-deception and self-justification, to recognize their root sin? Can God do that work? Remember, Satan said, "I am going throughout the world considering your works." Can God do that? Look how argumentative Job's friends are, how self-defensive they are. Try doing that to anybody, including a Christian. Suggest that they haven't gotten something right and be ready for the storm that will come back on you. Now, sometimes it is justified. I don't want anyone to go out and be a bunch of busybodies. They should receive a storm then. But even when it is needed and they say, "Hey, you haven't quite repented," they have to brace themselves from the storm that will come back, the storm of self-defensiveness. So how does God get that change to come about? If we are Eliphaz, we view all this suffering as for correction and discipline. It is soul-making. And if we raise any questions, we are questioning the sovereignty of God.

In 4:8-16, Eliphaz goes over seven forms of natural evil that God will deliver us from. He stays at that level, not getting any sense yet of the spiritual death that God is delivering us from. He says God is delivering us from natural evil. We are under natural evil for discipline; if we repent we'll be out of natural evil. Would not we like an easy life? I'd like to have an easy life.

Job Replies to Eliphaz: Does Eliphaz Have Knowledge?

Job replies in chapter 6, beginning by noting his condition. "If only my anguish could be weighed and all my misery be placed on the scales" (6:1). This is a counterexample to Eliphaz, who hasn't considered the depth of the problem. It is not just that Job is suffering; it is the depth of his suffering. This kind of suffering breaks Eliphaz's simple formula. It is too much. It is over the top. "It would surely outweigh the sand of the sea. No wonder my words have been impetuous" (6:2). So, Job gives a counterexample that Eliphaz is not able to put into his formula, which one must do if one is going to give an answer. This amount of suffering is over the top, it is too much. Eliphaz professes to believe in God, but when people in the world reject God with the problem of evil, they will point to serious problems that have happened that seem to go way beyond soul-making. There is too much suffering.

As Job draws attention to this, his request is to be cut off. That would make more sense if his sin had been so bad, and he would still have this: that he had not denied the words of God. So he asks for that: if his sin is this bad, then he should just be cut off. This is the same problem we saw in chapter three. His problem is to make sense of his suffering, to find meaning in it, in verses 8-10: "Oh, that I might have my request, that God would grant what I hope for, that God would be willing to crush me, to let loose his hand and cut me off. Then I would still have this consolation, my joy in unrelenting pain: that I had not denied the words of the Holy One." So how do we make sense of all this suffering in his life?

In verse 14, Job gets into his friends. A despairing man should have the devotion of his friends, even if he forsakes the fear of the Almighty. What do we expect out of friends when we are suffering? Do we expect them to rally around and help us? Do we expect them to love us? These friends, I think, are closer than the superficial view. They are not just bringing over some food or taking him out to a movie to get his mind off it. They are speaking about God and suffering—natural evil. Is not that what love requires? So, this is a ratcheted-up level, pressing us to see that their solution is emptiness still, because the friends don't have a full understanding of God in place. We need to see what that is exactly. Starting in 17:23, Job goes into what he had asked of his friends—he never asked anything from them.

He wants them to go beyond platitudes. "Teach me and I'll be quiet. Show me where I've been wrong." Remember Eliphaz began with that: it is your turn to be taught. So Job is saying, all right—teach me. At the very beginning of this section he already undermined Eliphaz's formula (the amount of my suffering destroys your formula) and he says, okay, if you can teach me, do it.

Job Wants Meaning

Job tries again to describe his condition. "Does not man have hard service on earth? Are not his days like those of a hired man, like a slave longing for the evening shadows, or a hired man waiting eagerly for his wages?" (v1-2). Job has had many months of futility and nights of misery. Another way it is summarized is this: life is full of misery and wickedness. Given this reality of suffering, immortality would be a curse. Job says in 7:6 that he is coming to an end without hope, and hope is one of the themes here. But in 7:16 he says, "I despise my life. I would not live forever. Let me alone. My days have no meaning." Wouldn't that be awful, to live forever without meaning? We wouldn't do that to even our enemies. Spiritual death forever. Job recognizes that. He is looking for meaning, and he is going to see if his friends can provide him with that.

He answers the question, why does God pay attention to him? He is going to undo the formula again. He is concluding his first response. Is God doing this to correct us? "Why does God pay attention to us?" Job asks, responding to that argument. "What is man that you make so much of him, that you give him so much attention, that you examine him every morning and test him every moment? Will you never look away from me, or let me alone for an instant?" (7:17). Just give me a break. If I have sinned, what have I done to you, O watcher of men? Why does God care about these things, about sin? Why have you made me your target? Why have I become a burden to you? Why do you not pardon my offenses and forgive my sins? "For I'll soon lie down in the dust. You'll search for me, but I'll be no more" (7:21). Our life is so short. God doesn't have better things to do?

Job wants meaning and he is getting closer. And his life is beautiful—with this development in the three friends and in Job, getting more and more focused on the problem, their dullness is coming out more and more and that gets more focused. But here Job focuses: my days have no meaning. Why do you pay attention to me? What have I done to you? That is going to be answered. What has Job done to God?

Bildad Round 1: Tradition

In chapter 8 Bildad steps in. He is different than Eliphaz. He is the type who finds comfort in the orthodoxy of the past. He has a nose for error and he rebukes Job more directly. His speech has three parts: first describing Job's condition, then explaining the authoritative view of suffering (*the* authoritative view, not simply his view), and then admonishing Job. Bildad focuses more in thinking about advice from himself. He is aware of himself; he is dealing a little more psychologically. He asks Job how long he will speak in this way with words that are empty. It is interesting, because I have been saying we should not empty our words of meaning. Bildad says, "Don't empty your words. How long will you say such things? Your words are a blustering wind. Does God pervert justice?" (8:1).

Remember that formula—Bildad still has that in the back of his mind—if you are innocent, you will not suffer. You are suffering, so you are not innocent. You are saying God perverts justice, Job. Obviously, you've done something wrong. Look at you. And then—feel this— "When your children sinned against him, he gave them over to the penalty of their sin." Is that pretty direct? "But if you look to God and plead with the Almighty, if you are pure and upright, even now, he will arouse himself on your behalf and restore you to your rightful place" (8:5-6). How nice of Bildad. When your children sinned, He killed them. But turn around and confess your sins to God.

The next section, 8:8-19, is a look at what tradition has told us. What does orthodoxy say? Ask the former generations and find out what their fathers learned. "But we were born only yesterday and know nothing, and our days on earth are but a shadow." Bildad is turning to tradition. What has the tradition told us? Will they not instruct you and tell you? Will they not bring forth words from their understanding? He goes through these things, this turning back to what we have been told about this problem. We have been told what happens to those who forget God and the suffering they come under. But we have also been told that God does not reject the blameless. Verse 20: "Surely God does not reject the blameless man or strengthen the hands of evildoers." That is obvious. That is what we have been taught in all the history of thought. "He will yet fill your mouth with laughter and your lips with shouts of joy. Your enemies will be clothed in shame" (8:21-22). Do we know a Bildad? Maybe he thinks that in his directness, he is just telling it like it is. Do we know someone like that? "I am sorry, I can't tell a lie." Don't ask them how your hair looks. "I can't tell a lie. I am pious, I am too pure for that." But Bildad is tactless. Out of his lack of understanding, he has a special cut to Job. That is not honesty. That is not the whole truth.

Job Replies to Bildad: Is the Formula Correct?

Job's response to Bildad continues his theme of the need for meaning. "Indeed, I know that this is true. How can a mortal be righteous before God? Though one wishes to speak with him, he could not answer him one time out of a thousand. His wisdom is profound; his power is vast" (9:2-4). Job says that, then he begins to get into God's creation. One could ask, how is this going to be different than what God says later? Because then Job begins to talk about what the creation says of God. "Even if I summoned him and he responded, I do not believe he would give me a hearing. He would crush me with a storm and multiply my words for no reason. He would not let me regain my breath. He would overwhelm me with misery. If it is a matter of strength, he is mighty. If it is a matter of justice, who will summon him? Even if I were innocent, my mouth would condemn me. If I were blameless, it would pronounce me guilty" (9:20). God does all he wants, including, Job says, destroying both the innocent and the wicked. All indeed die.

Bildad sort of continued the argument or the formula Eliphaz gave; now Job is responding to it: the good do die. People sing about how they die young. In your formula, Eliphaz, that makes no sense because good people do suffer. We are going to have to do better than Eliphaz's formula. If you're good, you would not die. You're dying, so you aren't good. And people will immediately say, what about babies? Every time. And we have got to be able to answer that. Why doesn't that question occur to Bildad? Job ends up having to do all the work in this dialogue. None of the others do that kind of thoughtful work of thinking about what questions they are bringing. And when Job points it out, they get angry. Bildad was very direct here; just wait till later, after he is heard Job respond to him and he expects Job to listen to him.

What is God's Purpose? Is There a Mediator?

What is the purpose of God in all of this? This is the question from Job I want to focus on. What is God's purpose in all of this? It does not make sense. It does not fit that neat formula of piety. Job begins to lament his inability to address God. Here's a theme that begins in this response. Job is going to ask for a mediator. Wouldn't it be nice if someone could address God for me? Anyone who has ever needed a lawyer knows what that is. We have seen these lawyer commercials: I'll fight for you. We don't want a sluggish, slothful lawyer who's barely able to energize himself. We want one who will fight for us, who knows the ins and outs of the system and who's on top of it. We think, maybe I'll get in there, I'll fumble my words, I won't know what I want to say...Wouldn't it be nice to have a mediator, someone to defend us? And in the language here, throughout the book, there is a legal structure: accusation and defender. Job asks for a defender, a mediator.

Job says in 9:32, "God is not a man like me that I might answer him, that we might confront each other in court. If only there were someone to arbitrate between us, to lay his hand upon us both, someone to remove God's rod from me so that his terror would frighten me no more. Then I would speak up without fear of him.

But as it now stands with me, I cannot." What is that mediator? Who is he going to be? What did Job understand about the sacrifices he was giving in the beginning? What's the purpose of sacrifices? We'll get to his understanding. Job's understanding is being deepened in this dialogue, which is suffering on top of suffering. "I loathe my very life. Therefore, I will give free reign to my complaint and speak out in the bitterness of my soul. I will say to God, 'Do not condemn me, but tell me what charges you have against me.'" That theme is coming up. What charges do you have against me? What have I done to deserve this?

There are two important parts. The "this" in its magnitude escapes Eliphaz. Look how bad this suffering is. And what have I done that would ever deserve this? What have I done to God that would deserve this? Why does God care about my faults? And it is going to be interesting. The benediction says, "May the love of God the Father be with you." Does God the Father love Job?

I want to get us ready for when we come to what God says. Job turns to the works of God the Creator. God created Job. Job asks, "What is God's purpose in all this?" In 10:8 he says, "Your hands shaped me and made me. Will you now turn and destroy me? Remember, you molded me like clay. Will you now turn me to dust again?... If I sin, you'll be watching me and will not let my offense go unpunished. If I am guilty, woe to me. Even if I am innocent, I cannot lift my head." So he is going to be asking us, what is this thing that I have done? And that is what's going to get Job into some trouble: being willing to defend himself at the expense of God. We'll look at how close he gets to crossing the line in defending himself. When does he come to see his root sin? That insight is what is going to fit things into place for him.

Zophar Round 1: Repent of Your Sin

Now we come to Zophar. Going back to 10:18, Job said, "Why even exist?" Sometimes he will talk as if he wants to die, but then he will say, "Why did you even bring me out of the womb? I wish I'd died before any eyes saw me." What's the purpose of existing? What's the meaning of it all? How well have we wrestled with that question ourselves? Perhaps we have been given a very easy life, and that is why I said earlier that an "easy" life, in terms of the history of the world, is the kind of life we live now. Again, we must consider: are we sure we want to be taught? What does Job have to go through to be taught?

So, then there is Zophar. Bildad was kind of a traditional guy, referring back to tradition and then applying it: here's the tradition; do it. Zophar, however, is business-minded and direct. He doesn't have time or patience for airy discussions, but wants to know, how does all this play out in the real world? He had be a good guy to have on a committee. Have you ever been in committee work and people just discuss, discuss, discuss forever? We want a guy who says, how does this work out? Let's just apply this. What does this do? But he lacks something we described earlier: he lacks the ordinary kindness, the milk of human kindness. He is good because he keeps those honest who are given to abstract navel gazing. But woe to those who fall into his hands. He is unable to see his own assumptions or consider counterexamples.

In the discussion, when those counterexamples get brought up with Job, Zophar loses his patience. He would say, "You sinned; repent. Just do it. Pound on the table. It is obvious. Do it." Do we know anybody like that? Have we been like that? What's obvious to Zophar may not actually be obvious because he may be objectively wrong.

His speech is pretty direct at the beginning of chapter 11: "Are these words to go unanswered? Is this talker to be vindicated? Will your idle talk reduce men to silence? Will no one rebuke you when you mock? You say to God, 'My beliefs are flawless and I am pure in your sight'." This is not quite what Job said. "Oh how I wish that God would speak. Then he would open his lips against you and disclose to you the secrets of wisdom, for true wisdom has two sides. Know this: God has even forgotten some of your sin." I love Zophar—look at that. You're wicked, he says to Job. You're so sinful, God has forgotten some of your sin, and he is still doing this to you, because of how much sin is left. That is what a sinner you are. If he comes along, and can find you in prison and convenes a court, who can oppose him? Surely, he recognizes deceitful men.

What is Zophar talking about? God recognizes deceitful men and takes care of them. He is taking care of you, Job. Therefore, you're a wicked, deceitful man. Yet there is hope for you, Job, "if you devote your heart to him and stretch out your hands to him; if you put away the sin that is in your hand and allow no evil to dwell in your tent, then you will lift up your face without shame. You will stand firm and without fear; you will surely forget your trouble, recalling it only as waters go by." Then he goes on to verse 20: "But the eyes of the wicked will fail, and escape will elude them. Their hope will become a dying gasp." Zophar thinks it is very easy. Job just needs to repent of his sins. Zophar is practical so he does not see the problem here. In his view a person does not need all this abstract thinking and wrestling through ideas. Job is a sinner and a really bad one; he should repent. That is a pretty direct, straightforward, and easy-to-understand equation.

Job's Reply and the End of Round 1

Then Job replies. This is the end of round one: "Doubtless you are the people and wisdom will die with you. No doubt you know everything. But I have a mind as well as you" (v2-3a). I am not inferior to you, Job says. Who does not know all these things? There is a truthfulness to the form that has been given. This formula is accurate. God is sovereign and God is good and God is just and God does deal that way with the wicked. Who does not know those things? Job knows all those same things. He starts in verse 7 with another example from creation. And then in 13, he goes over the sovereignty of God. And I want to warn you, a very common reading of the book is that Job has questions, God shows up and says, "I am sovereign," and Job is silent. And that is not so common as to be unbelievable, but it is not consistent with what is here. Job already knows God is sovereign. His three friends and Job, all four of them, talk about the sovereignty of God. So, what is the problem here? What's going on? Verse 13: "My eyes have seen all this. My ears have heard and understood it. What you know, I also know. I am not inferior to you. But I desire to speak to the Almighty and to argue my case with God."

Zophar did not get to sin in his dialogue. And I think it is because he hadn't gotten to sin in his own life. He is probably one of these very pious rule followers; he keeps the rules and views himself as having done that. He would not be able to give a very good testimony. He may have been brought up in church and kept all the rules since his youth. He never did anything wrong. He fell from the womb a Christian. And so, when he sees Job suffering, he says: "You. Look at you." One can't help but hear the spirit of the Pharisee here, praying at the temple: My prayer is just that I am so thankful I am not that guy. That is my whole prayer: that I am not like that sinner next to me, like Job.

Then Job has this line in 13:4: "You, however, smear me with lies. You are worthless physicians, all of you." Worthless physicians. These men are brought to us as the height of wisdom at the time. These three guys represent persons who are known for their wisdom. They are given titles at the beginning. And they are worthless physicians. They don't have wisdom. They don't understand. They cannot argue Job's case. He wants someone who will argue his case, and they are not able to be the mediator he is looking for. He says in 13:6, "Hear now my argument and listen to the plea of my lips." And he wants someone who will do that for him. Then he says in 15: "Though he slay me, yet I will hope in him. I will surely defend my ways to his face." He has this juxtaposition of trusting God; his hope is in God, God is good, but he wants to argue his case. What sin is it that I have committed?

Job Addresses God

Then in 13:20 it shifts from addressing the friends to addressing God. His friends have so utterly failed, so Job directs his attention now to God and addresses God directly. "Only grant me these two things, oh God, and then I will not hide from you. Withdraw your hand far from me, and stop frightening me with your terrors. Then summon me and I will answer you." He continues to address God in v14: "Man born of woman is of few days and full of trouble." This is the human condition. I can't help but hear Psalm 90 in the next few verses. 14:7: "At least there is hope for a tree; if you cut it down it might sprout again. But what hope is there for us?"

We have these themes in Job: he wants to have his integrity. He can't make sense of what's been happening to him, and he believes he does still keep his integrity, but in this condition, what hope do we have—especially if we can't make any sense of what's been happening to us? So in verse 13 he says: "If only you would hide me in the grave and conceal me till your anger has passed. If only you would set me a time and then remember me." Verse 15: "You will call and I will answer you. You will long for the creature your hands have made. Surely then you will count my steps, but not keep track of my sin. My offenses will be sealed up in a bag; you will cover over my sin." This is coming to two parts. Sometimes Job is talking and doesn't seem to say he has sinned, but other times he will talk about his sins, yet he will point out: in what way are they a bother to God? Why does God care about my sins? What are they to him that he is paid this kind of attention to me? The answer he gets is going to address both of those things.

In what sense has Job sinned? He is blameless. And in what way does that sin affect God at all? Through all of this, what is God doing, and what is it going to take to bring Job to see God's works? Why couldn't God have just given him a scroll at the beginning with the answer in it? That is the glory of God that we are seeing displayed here. This trial is not just for Job, but Job goes through it in a specific way, a kind of depth that we don't see elsewhere. The reason is partly—or precisely—because he is blameless. That is why each of us should not worry about going through what he does—we are not blameless. All this happened to Job because he is blameless. And God will bring him through this and we'll see what it takes for him to break through to greater understanding.

Job's Understanding Is Being Pressed

Job is going further down the road in this first round of blaming God. We have been introduced to all three friends, and we should get to know them because we might start to notice them around us. We can hang out with our friends and say, "You're such a Bildad." "Oh—well, I was going to say *you* are. It is funny you saw that in me. You have no tact." As we start to get to know these characters, we recognize the traits that come together with them. Why are they engaged in counterexamples themselves and seeing their own assumptions? So, rather than just doing an informative discussion of Job, the book presses us to ask, do we know ourselves? And do we really want to know ourselves? We like to say, I know myself. I think that is a lie. Because if we wanted to know ourselves, we would know ourselves. We are not contending with the reality of self-deception and self-justification. And what's it going to take for God to break through those things? And how much will that work? Can we see that work in our own life? And that is part of what's wonderful about thinking of our own testimony, considering our own root sin that all of us have in common.

We don't have fruit sin in common, but we all have root sin in common. It i's the same for us and the same for blameless, patient Job. And this suffering is what it takes to get our attention. Do we believe that? This is what it takes to get our attention. This is what it took to get Job's attention. Patient, blameless Job—it took this. Yet woe to us if we don't pay attention even in this. Some don't. Let us not allow ourselves to be preoccupied, to be busy in mind and life so that we miss this and we lose our own vitality—we become lifeless—so that professing faith, we are overall lifeless and not producing fruit. We need to repent of that root sin individually and corporately if we expect there to be that kind of reviving in ourselves. We pray for that in ourselves and pray for that in the church. We pray for that life God gives by his Spirit that will enable us to see God with our own heart. Round one has ended.

Job Part Three

I Know My Redeemer Lives

19:25-26
I know that my redeemer lives, and that in the end he will stand on the earth. And after my skin has been destroyed, yet in my flesh I will see God.

"And although after my skin worms destroy this body, yet in my flesh shall I see God." This is from Handel's Messiah; it is one of the best-known parts of Handel's Messiah. "I know that my redeemer lives." This comes roughly in the middle of the second round of speeches as Job responds this time to the second speech from Bildad. It is kind of a dialogue—though these might feel more like speeches than a dialogue. Usually we don't go on and on for paragraphs at somebody when we are in a dialogue. The way it is structured is more like speeches, but it is dialogue in the sense that the speeches are building on each other; they are responding to each other. This is roughly in the middle of that second round.

Round Two: The Biblical Worldview

Job is with his comforters. He is not yet at the end of the book, where he is able to say to God, "Now my eyes have seen you" (42:5). He has more struggle ahead of him and more that needs to be brought out of him and exposed. The struggle is with his comforters, but it is also with himself. So how does he come to say this here? Because this seems to be a great confession of faith. How many can say, "I know my redeemer lives and that although I die, I will see him in the flesh"? This shows something of the faith of Job right here in the middle of the book; that very faith which is being tested. How does he know this? That is what stood out to me here. I *know* that my redeemer lives. Job does not say, I believe my redeemer lives; I have been told my redeemer lives. Those are all different than I *know* my redeemer lives. How can he say such a strong thing? How did he come to know that? Would we like to know how Job came to know that? And would we like to know it ourselves in the same way?

To understand this, we are going to remind ourselves a little bit about the context of the book of Job. As I have said before, as we come to the book of Job, we have the Biblical worldview in place. We are looking at it from that perspective. As I am reading commentaries on the book of Job, they come from every angle one can imagine. I am going to mention Jung's commentary today, just by way of dismissal. Anticipate what's in that one: the gnostic reading of Job.

We are approaching Job from the biblical worldview. We already have that in place, but sometimes some of the questions we might bring up about Job are really questions about that biblical worldview. Especially if someone might say that in these verses, Anderson is imposing Christianity. He is doing a Christian reading of Job, and that is not faithful to the text. We want to respond to challenges—and see if I am doing a "Christian reading of Job." I think if we read Job, we'd use the same principles Peter used in Acts when he explained the sacrifice: that the sacrifice had always been a sign of what we should have expected. We can use similar principles when we think about Job and his sacrifices, what he was offering. We already have the biblical worldview in place. We don't need to argue for that here, but we can set out some of the key pieces: that the creation clearly reveals God.

There are three parts: that the creation reveals; that it is clear; and knowing who God is. We don't need to question in the book that God is perfect in power and knowledge and goodness. We come to the book with that assumption. So, for example, Jung says something along the lines of this: "Job had a lot to learn, but so did Yahweh." No. We come to Job knowing that is not true. We don't need to defend that out of the book of Job. Jung's gnostic framework teaches that Yahweh is one of the gods and is like us in being temporal. We know from general revelation that God is eternal. Our highest good is to know God in all that by which he makes himself known. We come to the book knowing that, and that is true for all four of these characters in the book. And that is what God is working toward in Job's life: that God loves Job and wants that highest good for him.

We come to the book knowing that sin is a failure to seek, a failure to understand, and a failure to do what is right. We already know that about sin, and as we start to look for sin, we see the understanding of these three comforters, but we also see what they say is sin in Job. We know that natural evil is a callback from moral evil, so when we think about the suffering of Job here—the depth of his suffering—we have that framework in mind. It is not punishment. That understanding helps us as we deal with these three friends. We know that this sin in us requires atonement through the death of another. Job knew that. He is involved in offering sacrifices at the very beginning, so we know he understands that. He has the same understanding that Abel did. When people try to date the book of Job, they think that it matters in terms of what he understood of the sacrifice. Does he have access to Moses or not? That does not matter. He has access to the same thing Abel did. And we are aware of our need for justification and sanctification and how those differ, and that matters as we look at the life of Job. For him, is sanctification going on or justification?

And then, of course, we naturally want to say, well, what about me? How do I apply this to my life, my family's life? We need to be reminded all the time of each of those truths as we struggle to keep them in focus in our minds, as we struggle to interpret our own lives and our own circumstances. How easily our focus is shifted, isn't it? We have to remind ourselves, just like we daily eat bread.

No one would say, well, I fed my body four months ago; I am good. It is almost one of the main topics of the day, isn't it? Oh, what should we have for breakfast? Oh, what should we have for lunch? Oh, what should we have for dinner? Oh, what should we have for breakfast? They just repeat. It should be like that with the bread of life. Oh, have I had the bread of life today? Have I had the word of God? Have I reminded myself of these principles or do I do intermittent bread-of-life-fasting? Sixteen hours of fasting? No, about four or five months fasting. It makes you lean. No, it does not work—not for spiritual purposes.

It is not uncommon to get lost in the middle of Job. We get excited, we love this story, it is one of the best-known stories, we get into it, and we have got heavenly powers involved...then we get into some of the lamenting, and we say, yeah, I am just like Job. I really relate. And then it starts going into the chapters and it gets a little daunting and we might get lost. Who's saying what? Wait, Bildad just said God is just—that is true—but I thought Bildad was the bad guy. So, we can start to get lost in the middle and it can be hard to keep track of the responses and the flow and process of ideas. It is like reading through the one-year Bible and getting stuck by the time we get to Leviticus. So that is part of what I am trying to help us do in this book—not just enjoy the beginning and end, but also this middle part, and see the development that is going on, because understanding and learning how to interpret that will help us in interpreting our own lives.

Inner Thoughts Exposed

What we are seeing here is the inner thoughts being exposed. We all have those secret intents of the

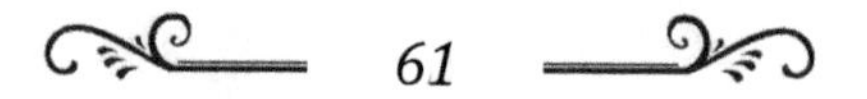

heart; how we understand the world. And what usually comes out is the way we are interacting with each other. I don't mean this in a pejorative sense, but it is kind of a superficial sense. We don't immediately get into the deepest things of our hearts; it is not the right time for that. But in these kinds of circumstances, that is what comes out. And for each of these three characters and Job, that is coming out. How do you understand the world when the crisis happens? And these three guys are called upon to comfort their friends. I am using that term on purpose. We could maybe say the word friends as well. What would it be to comfort someone? That happens with all of us: as we go through a trial, our inner thoughts come out and are exposed, and that is part of what the curse is for. So, what we are going to see and what we are seeing in Job is: what does it take to overcome self-deception and self-justification? What will it take to learn humility and to examine ourselves? As our thoughts come out, they meet resistance; they harden by becoming more consistent.

In the second round we see that all three of these comforters get hardened in their response; they become more adamant against Job. Now, there is usually no problem in getting someone to want to be "honest with themselves." People love to talk about themselves. Dale Carnegie said that is the way to win friends and influence people. Get them to talk about themselves. Ask them about their opinions. They love to tell you their opinions. "Well, I am glad you asked; let me tell you." But that is not the same as actually confronting our self-deception. What we are doing then is we are being honest about your self-deception. We are not calling the self-deception, but we are being sincere, expressing where we are at in self-deception. Job is telling us what it is going to take to get through that. Did you really understand chapter three of Genesis and what it is going to take—what the curse means? This is what it looks like. It is pretty intense. This is the problem of self-deception about ourselves. What will it take for us to see this? And these speeches or dialogues are showing that in each of these persons.

The personalities of Eliphaz and Bildad and Zophar came out in how they responded to Job. And now we pick up in chapter 15 with Eliphaz again. He was initially more refined and spoke from his own experience and gave advice based on what he would do in that situation. And he is the one who articulated the formula that they are all working out of: the innocent do not suffer. And when we say refined, what I mean is, he leaves it there for Job to fill it in. Because what's the implication? He came to comfort Job, who's suffering greatly. And Eliphaz says, the innocent do not suffer. Whereas, by contrast, Bildad particularly, is more direct: the wicked, like you, suffer. So, they are saying the same things, but Eliphaz is more careful in one way. He also likes to talk out of his own experience. "You know, if it were me, here's what I would do." That is how he speaks. And remember the centrality of that religious experience for him—the spirit who came to him at night shaped his whole understanding of this process. He did not test the spirit. "Oh, but that is a Christian thing to do." No, that is a general revelation thing to do. Don't believe every voice you hear. So that is Eliphaz.

Bildad appeals to tradition and what has come down to us as the answer about how God works. What have the wise told us? We all know the following. And because of that, he is very confident and very direct about what he says. I am laying out these personalities because we might meet people like these. When we look in the mirror, we might meet one of them. They are greeting each of us. So Bildad is more confident because he is sure that he is speaking out of the accumulated wisdom of the world. And so, he can be direct. "It's not me speaking; it's the wise, and they've told us this."

Zophar is more action-oriented, and he has a kind of appeal to common sense. "Just repent. You clearly sinned. Repent of your sin! It is common sense—look at what's happening to you."

These personalities continue into the second discourse, but they are hardened. We'll look at what that means. Each person, including Job, develops in their view as the discussion presses them to be more consistent with their beliefs. And that is the process I want us to pay attention to, to help give meaning to this part of the book and how that happens in our own life: these hidden thoughts of the heart come out. Our thoughts can be hardened, and suffering brings them out. Will they be able to get back to their basic beliefs and get them in focus in their mind to evaluate them? If they don't, they've wasted their suffering. And if it does happen, that will be the turning point. Remember, Job is concerned about integrity. Satan said to God, he will curse you to your face; Job only loves God for what he gets. We are going to see: is that true of Job? His integrity has been challenged by Satan, and Job does not know that part, but he knows that his integrity is being questioned by these events. And his friends are going to call it into question very directly. So why is this integrity so important to Job?

Eliphaz: Wisdom and Vanity

In chapter 15, Eliphaz sets out and begins this discourse. "Would a wise man answer with empty notions or fill his belly with the hot east wind? Would he argue with useless words, with speeches that have no meaning?" He begins by asking, what is a wise person? And true to Eliphaz, he gives a formula for us. He is right, isn't he? Do we want to talk with someone whose words are empty? The word for empty is "vanity." This is like saying we need common ground to have conversation. And formally speaking, that is true. So, we have to look at the content that he is going to put into that. If you're wise, do you utter vanity? No.

So again, here's the roundabout way Eliphaz is speaking to Job: you're speaking vanity. If you were wise, you would not speak vanity; therefore, you are not wise. Whereas we might see Bildad being willing to say directly, you are not wise. Emptiness, purposelessness, meaninglessness, nonsense. These are all cognates of vanity. Do we want to talk with someone who's uttering those things, contrasted to wisdom?

The application is important. It is not enough to go around telling people that we need common ground and repeating that over and over. We need to use reason and have meaning in our words. Eliphaz can say that. The content is what is important. The application of this is what is important. And has Job done that? He is being challenged now. Is it true that he is speaking in vanity? That is what these dialogues are exposing. That is why, as we get into the book, that is the exciting part to see.

People like to watch fights. There are major fights and even presidents attend to see who is going to win. So here we have an intellectual fight; both sides are telling the other one that they are speaking empty, meaningless words. After making that kind of general point, Eliphaz does not say "Job" or "you" in chapter 15 verses 1, 2, and 3. In 4, he gets into this: "Would you even undermine piety?" That is how the NIV says it. Or in the King James: "You cast off fear and restraineth prayer before God." I like that better. I like the King James' phrasing better, because that gets to the key of wisdom better. "You've cast off the fear of God," Eliphaz tells Job. That is getting to it; that is very direct. Job does not fear God. As I said before, that used to be a kind of name for Christians. Are you a God-fearer? Or do you go about your life? If you fear something, you do something about whatever you are fearing. So if someone has a kind of lazy attitude about whatever, they don't have fear related to it.

If you are a God-fearer, you would repent before God. You would recognize your need for God. And he says, "Your own mouth condemns you." And then he goes into an explanation of why that is in verse 7, and what his basis is for saying that. Your own mouth condemns you. This is his response to Job's speech. They are not getting anywhere. That is what we mean by hardening. He does not say to Job, you've made some good points; let me think about that. "Your own mouth condemns you." Are you the first man who was ever born? Were you brought forth before the hills? Do you listen in on God's counsel? Do you limit wisdom to yourself? Who are you that you think so highly of your wisdom? And in contrast to you, the gray-haired and the aged are on our side. We are much older than you, older than your father; our wisdom comes from that, and you should listen to us.

This is a charge of pride in Job. Job is proud and vain, Eliphaz says. And that is a development from his earlier rhetoric—Eliphaz is getting sharper. That is what I mean by hardened. Who are you to question these things, Job? Don't question what God is doing. So, the discussion produces a kind of revision of his formula that the innocent don't suffer. It is the problem of evil, but phrased in that way.

Now Eliphaz says in 15:14, "What is man that he could be pure, or one born of woman, that he could be righteous?" He is going to shift now, and I think he is saying something more along the lines of: to be human is to be a miserable sinner. So why are you, Job, surprised about what's happened to you? That is a little bit of a different emphasis, and especially when we get to Zophar and see how he develops that. Verse 17: "Listen to me and I'll explain to you." Let me tell you what I have seen. That was Eliphaz's attitude: "Here's what I would do in a situation." So here he is, back with the same personality. To be born human is to be a sinner. Does being human help us get out of stuff? "I am only human; why are you holding me to such a difficult standard?"

Then Eliphaz shifts to this personal experience—a very similar pattern as the first time around. "Let me show you what I have been through. This is what happened." Incidentally, I like how this works. He says this: let me tell you what I have seen; and then what he goes on to say also happens to line up with what wise people say. Verse 18: "This is what wise men have declared." And here's his formula in verse 20: "All his days, the wicked man suffers torment, the ruthless through all the years stored up for him." The focus in this second section is on the wicked. He had phrased it as the innocent the first time around. Now it is on the wicked. All the days of the wicked, they suffer.

Do the Wicked Actually Suffer?

As we get into their arguments, do we think that is true? We can reflect in our mind, and cast our minds into the thinking of someone who's wicked. Do they suffer all their days? What happens to the wicked? Well, according to Eliphaz they have an awful life. Eliphaz goes through and names a number of these things here. And he especially gets to this in verse 23 (NIV): "He wanders about, food for vultures." Whereas the King James says, "He wanders about looking for food." "He knows the day of his darkness is at hand; distress and anguish fill him with terror. They overwhelm him like a king poised to attack because he shakes his fist at God." And in verse 27 to the end of that section: "All that he is built, all that he is done, will come to ruin and naught. He has deceived himself by trusting in what is worthless." And then in verse 33, "He will be like a vine stripped of its unripe grapes, like an olive tree shedding its blossoms, for the company of the godless will be barren, and fire will consume the tents of those who love bribes. They conceive trouble and give birth to evil; their womb fashions deceit." The life of the wicked comes to nothing. Fruitless. A barren womb. And it cannot have missed Job that his children had all just died. He is barren. That is the outcome of the wicked. And we think back on those songs of lament as well. So Job should stop fighting. He is fighting against the wise.

Job Too Has Studied

In 16: Job also can think and observe. He, too, has studied what's been said. He begins it this way: "I have heard many such things—miserable comforters are you all!" What would it be to comfort somebody? Job's comforters are more like accusers. There is a kind of legal or court structure to the book, and they are accusing him of these things. And he is been accused by Satan. Think of how they add to his suffering—the physical torment of Job is increased by this spiritual torment. Which would be worse? The accusation—not only are you suffering, but you're wicked. You're suffering because you deserve it due to that wickedness—and you're an unrepentant sinner. We can think of the torment heaped on Christ. "He trusted in God—let him deliver him if he delights in him." How that torment, that accusation, adds to it. Job too has this. "I also could speak like you" (v4). What would it take to comfort someone? Comfort is connected to hope. It is about connecting up hope to knowing and understanding. And wouldn't it have been nice for Job's friends to have brought that comfort to him? Can we comfort others? Can we comfort ourselves? Comfort, comfort ye my people. What would bring comfort to the people of God? Job cries out and asks for that; comfort from the physical and spiritual torment that he is in. He says, "I can make fine speeches like you and shake my head like you, but my mouth would encourage you. Comfort from my lips would bring you relief. Yet if I speak, my pain is not relieved, and if I restrain, it does not go away" (v6). Why continue this dialogue if it is not helping, not getting to what he needs?

I think there is something self-referential here. If Job really is speaking empty words, why is Eliphaz still talking to him, based on his own principle that it is worthless to talk to someone who's speaking empty words? So, this is beginning to reveal some of the lack of wisdom on their part. Verses 4 and 5 in chapter 16 contrast what they are doing with how Job would bring comfort. And in verse 6, he specifically mentions his grief. Neither speaking nor remaining silent helps with his grief. Grief especially is a kind of mental suffering caused by loss. Grief is that loss we might feel in life. Loss of goods, like in the psalms. If we lose our job, lose our spouse, lose our health. How about lose our meaning? Oh, I misplaced my meaning. I need to get one of those beepers for my meaning, and it is an app on my phone and if I touch it, it beeps. What would we do without meaning in life in trying to make sense of the world? This is what Job is wrestling with—meaning and understanding, and that is related to his integrity. It is very painful to go from thinking we understand to an absolute loss of this and facing meaninglessness. People argue about very superficial things and they don't like being told they don't understand those things. We can think of sports and say, oh, the best team ever is this team. What? No, it isn't. It is clearly this other team. The best sport is this one. No, it obviously isn't. It is this other one. So, imagine that about the meaning of life itself. We have gone along confidently in life thinking we understood how things work, and then bam—we are confronted with what we did not understand this whole time and we lose that meaning that is in our life. That is what is meant by the phrase "existential crisis." How would we fare going through that? It is one thing when we are young; have we prepared for crises? It is another thing as we are older and we are already going through those.

In 16:7 Job shifts his focus from his friends to God. In one way, that begins a pattern here: there is less and less to talk about with his friends. "Surely, oh God, you have worn me out." God's sovereignty has been affirmed throughout the whole book by all four of them. So, the idea that this is somehow a process of coming to learn God's sovereignty is inaccurate—he already knew that coming into this whole situation. In verse 9, "God assails me and tears me in his anger and gnashes his teeth at me. My opponent fastens on me his piercing eyes." In verse 12, he had been at ease, but now he is broken. And in verses 15-17 Job responds to these: "I've sewn sackcloth over my skin and buried my brow in the dust." Sackcloth and ashes, sorrow and grief. In verse 17 Job says there is no justice; there is only injustice in his lot. His own hands have been free from violence and his prayer is pure. Remember, Eliphaz had said, you hinder prayer. He is countering that: my prayer is pure; I haven't been unjust.

A Mediator

Earlier in chapter 9, Job had asked for someone to arbitrate for him, and he returns to that in 16:19-21. "Even now, my witness is in heaven, my advocate is on high. My intercessor is my friend, and my eyes pour out tears to God. On behalf of a man he pleads with God as a man pleads for his friend." I want us to be equipped here to reason through it the way Job would have and avoid this criticism that we are bringing New Testament ideas to the book of Job. Job can reason the same way Adam and Abel, Noah and Abraham could have reasoned about the sacrifice, the coats of skin. Another is dying for me. That is a mediator or an intercessor. And this is how Peter argues in Acts: it can't just be an animal. It had to be a human. We'd know that from the fact of representation, just as one man brought sin into the world, all the way from Genesis 3. So, we would know that our intercessor would argue for us in our place—he would take our place. These are not simply Christian ideas imposed backwards. Just the opposite: it might be that Christians don't see it. It might be that Jesus himself had to tell the people: "you have been slow to understand all the things have been written about me in the scriptures." Does Jesus mean they have not understood the scriptures of the New Testament? No—Jesus is referring to the Old Testament.

Job concludes here: only the grave awaits him. He is surrounded by mockers. Those two go together. There is imagery here, anticipation of Christ surrounded by mockers. Christ trusted God. Remember Abel, who was hated for his sacrifice and murdered for it. So, these patterns come out.

In 17:2: "Mockers surround me; my eyes must dwell on their hostility." And in 17:3 Job asks for someone to give him surety or a pledge. Instead, he is been made a byword to everyone: a man of sorrows and acquainted with grief. We might say this is the Handel's Messiah. But we can see how numerous passages come out that highlight these themes. And Handel used some of these. Job is accustomed to this kind of treatment.

Then in 17:10: "But come on, all of you—try again. I will not find a wise man among you." Job can punch back. Where is wisdom? Comfort is connected to hope, and you friends have given no hope. What if the only hope we have is the grave? Job is asking for an answer in these verses, and without an answer, there is no understanding; there is just that vanity and meaninglessness that we keep coming back to. That is a condition of no hope. Of any book in the scriptures which will lament grief and loss, Lamentations should come to mind. And Jeremiah and Job are often compared to each other. Lamentations 2:20: "Look, oh Lord, and consider: whom have you ever treated like this? Should women eat their offspring, the children they have cared for? Should priest and prophet be killed in the sanctuary of the Lord? Young and old lie together in the dust of the streets. My young men and maidens have fallen by the sword. You have slain them in the day of your anger; you have slaughtered them without pity." Lamentations 3:1: "I am the man who has seen affliction by the rod of his wrath. He has driven me away and made me walk in darkness rather than light. Indeed, he has turned his hand against me again and again all day long." But then in the same chapter, verse 25: "The Lord is good to those whose hope is in him, to the one who seeks him.

It is good to wait quietly for the salvation of the Lord. It is good for a man to bear the yoke while he is young." These things are good. The things that are described are quite terrible, but the Lord is good to those who hope in him.

And Job is at that point; he is wrestling with "I have no hope but the grave." So there is a development here: I want to understand, I don't understand, and that understanding is what brings hope and brings comfort. And even Jeremiah sees this. I look at Jeremiah because of the depth of that suffering that is expressed in Lamentations. Jeremiah comes to say this: "It is good for a man to bear the yoke. We are to wait quietly for the salvation of the Lord."

So back to Job 17: Job's integrity. How many would continue on instead of just turning away at this point? There is a Babylonian Job, a text written maybe in the 8th century-ish, lamenting some very similar things. And it has a parallel because he has a friend to come and talk to him—one friend. And he goes through asking, why have the gods done this to me—the Babylonian gods? I've been a really good god-worshiper all this time. But at the end he says, I guess I just need to worship the gods more. I'll go extra. I'll go to Sunday morning *and* Sunday evening service for the gods. There is no growth in understanding at all in that Babylonian Job. Just a kind of doubling down on, I'll keep the rules even more—I'll double the rules. But Job is asking, where is there hope? Job 17:15: "Where then is my hope? Who can see any hope for me?" We'll go down to the gates of death. Will we descend together into dust? What hope do we have? We can't just say, hey, look, I think the stock market is going to turn around, Job. You'll be fine. What hope is there in knowing the purpose of any of this? Either way, we will come to the grave. And so Job ends his first round here with asking that exact question of his friends. He wants them to bring comfort, as opposed to accusations.

Bildad: We Too Have Wisdom

Then we have Bildad in chapter 18. Let's say our friend comes to us. He says, I need comfort. I am afflicted by God. Help me understand my hope. What do we say to our friend? It would be the most natural thing in the world, wouldn't it, to try to answer that? It is one thing if they are suffering and they did not ask for help. No one wants to be preached at when they are suffering. We are talking about a friend who comes to you and says, I am suffering; help me. Well, how does Bildad do it? He says, "When are you going to end these speeches? Be sensible and then we can talk." Is that what we would say to our friend? "Be sensible and then we can talk." Do you think that we are just mere beasts, that we don't understand? And Bildad lays right into it. Job ended with his plea, and Bildad just goes right into it: "Don't you think we have wisdom on our side as well?" This personality that has tradition on their side can be helpful in some circumstances, but is completely useless in these circumstances, because that is the person who will avoid heresy. They know the tradition. They are heresy hunters, they are called; they will make sure you haven't gone astray in any little way. And that is all good—keep me on the straight and narrow. Thank you. But when these conditions come up, this person will be of no use—in fact, they will be harmful.

Bildad continues his theme of the received wisdom of the ages. From 18:5-21 he describes what befalls the wicked, just like Eliphaz had. We can go through this and see if these things are true. Is this really what happens to the wicked? Job can look around also; he can observe. The lamp of the wicked is snuffed out, the flame of their fire stops burning. In verse 12, calamity is hungry for him; disaster is ready for him when he falls. It is part of the problem that this does not happen to the wicked. That is what Psalm 37 cautions us not to do because we will lay there in bed thinking, wow, the wicked get away with it; they seem to prosper. So, what is Bildad talking about?

In 18:19 Bildad says that the wicked has no offspring or descendants among his people, no survivor where he once lived. Then in verse 21: "Surely such is the dwelling of an evil man, such is the place for the man who knows not God." Again, he is addressing Job's situation. It can't be missed on Job that his children just died. That is got to be fresh on his mind. No hope, no future. People want there to be some sense in which they contributed to the world. Once I am gone, is my life like a sandcastle built by the waves, and they come in and completely erase it and one can never even know that the sandcastle had been there within two or three waves? Is that what our life is like? We want to have some sense of having fruit, whether physical or spiritual. That is what Gilgamesh wanted—will I be able to have my name live forever? Achilles wanted that. In other words, even sinners see that we should have something, some lasting contribution. And it is true that the wicked won't have a contribution; that they will be destroyed. Bildad is not wrong about that. How does Psalm 112 apply here? Job responds in chapter 19: how long will you torment me and crush me with your words? Remember Job's desire for fruit when we come to the end of the book.

Job's Comfort

Job had asked for comfort and hope; Bildad gives him a description of the painful, vain life of the wicked. If a friend comes and asks for comfort, should one give him a description of the wicked suffering? Is that comfort? Why have Job's friends made this any of their concern? "Ten times now you've approached me; shamelessly you attack me. If it is true that I have gone astray, my error remains my concern alone" (19:3-4). Why is it any of their business to add to these problems? Busybodies. Do we know busybodies that can make our problems their problems? So now Job is at this point: what you speak is nonsense. He asks, why have you made this your concern? You're not helping at all. If it is true that I have gone astray, then I'll have to deal with that.

In 19:6, Job shifts again to God. As I said, most of this ends up being directed at God. "Then know that God has wronged me and drawn his net around me." He is getting closer and closer now to accusing God. God has overthrown me, he says. We can look at these descriptions and compare them to what Bildad said would happen to the wicked. Bildad said, these things will befall the wicked, and then Job says, this is what's befallen me. The difference is, he is saying that his situation does not fit what Bildad says happens to the wicked. I haven't done the wicked things you're saying, Bildad, so your formula is false. It is a kind of empirical formula. These five things happen to the wicked; we'll go out into the world and look and see. Do those actually happen to the wicked? And we don't see that happening many times. It is what exasperates the righteous because they don't see that—they want to see them more swiftly happen.

So Bildad's supposed wisdom is simply incorrect. Job says, have pity on me. Have pity on me, my friends. He is received no pity and no comfort. Verse 21: "For the hand of God has struck me." He is coming once again to his friends. He finds no pity from them. They've abandoned him. And then in verse 23, Job begins the part I quoted earlier. He asks for his account to be written—his witness. He is using these court images again. It is a witness to his condition—a faithful witness of what he is gone through because these have been lying witnesses. And we can think about it from our vantage point, looking back, how this actually worked out in God's providence. At this time did Job have any idea we'd be talking about the book of Job? His witness was written in a way he would never have expected. And it is come down through the ages as not just a witness for Job, but also as a revelation of divine providence for all to see. And that is how all of providence is for each one of us.

Our lives reveal the faithful and tender love of God. Even when we are suffering, we can look to that and say what Job says: I know that my Redeemer lives. Job asked for that witness, and God does not let Job's suffering go to waste. If God cared to make sure Job's suffering doesn't go to waste, God cares that ours doesn't go to waste. We should use our suffering as part of the discipline of God in our lives. Don't allow it to go to waste. And interestingly, Job says in 24 that he does not want his witness to be lost. He says, I want it to be inscribed with an iron tool on lead or engraved in rock forever. So there is a sense of permanence. I can't help but think of the image of the rock in the Old Testament. Engraved in a rock. Is it just a metaphor, or a literal image of inscribing things on stone? Or is this engraved in The Rock forever? Who will be his advocate and bear those marks forever? Job says in19: 25, I know that my redeemer lives. And we laid out earlier how he could know that.

This is the term "kinsman redeemer." It is a very important concept in the book of Ruth. Boaz is her kinsman redeemer, the closest male relative who will redeem her from debt and loss. So that is not imposing something back on the text; that is what that term means. What else can Job know? Job can know that death was not original. The persons I read coming to this text were largely not believers, and they don't believe death was not original. Or if they are believers, they may be theistic evolutionists. Job can know that death was not original; that once moral evil is defeated, physical death is removed: the resurrection. Physical death is a callback from moral evil. Job can know that, just as Abel knew that. That is how Job can say, I know my redeemer lives. He would know that God provided the coats of skin. He would know that he was giving offerings for his children, and what those symbolized. That is how he can know. Rather than simply saying, I was catechized that my redeemer lives; I can give the correct answer to the question—we should say, I know it and I should build a response to challenges that come up. And that is what Job is doing.

These challenges have come up in Job's life, bringing him to wrestle with what he thought he understood. He would know that none of us can be that redeemer, just as he would know sin was not original and it came into the world through the act of Adam. That is representation. So, he would know that this redeemer is his representative, his advocate. That is the term he is using. He would have to be redeemed by someone who can represent us. And that is why he uses these phrases that show clearly this is going to be a human who represents us. Our redeemer is one of us. This test is getting these things into focus for Job. Let's let it do that for us also by reading through this. That is what the scholar's life was: sitting in a room surrounded by books, all the greatest books of world history. We say, now I will learn all about life just by sitting here and reading these books. Is that how it works? No, that is not how life works at all. This, in Job, is how life works. But we'd better have that knowledge as we are coming into this stuff.

Job would know about the seed of the woman crushing the head of the serpent. So although he does not know about Satan talking to God—those particular details of what Satan said (he will curse you to your face)—he would still know about the spiritual war. Would we like to hear Job's thoughts on the spiritual war? Job could have known all these things just as Abraham knew these things. I mention Abraham because he is the father of the faithful who reasoned that God could raise Isaac from the dead. Job could reason that same way. All humans can and should know these things. And hope, apart from knowledge, is false hope. He is asking for comfort. To have hope, it must be based on knowledge—I know my redeemer lives. How do we know that?

Job's hope has to transcend his own life and his own death and reach into the resurrection. This comfort can't just be someone saying, it will turn around; there are ups and downs; you're in a season of life. Well, I am going to die. That is the end of seasons. Our hope has to see that resurrection, like the eagle eye of Stephen, whose sight pierced beyond the grave and saw his Master. Can your eyes pierce beyond the grave to find that hope that is there? Hope is contrasted with a lack of understanding, a lack of desire to see God—a dull heart. Lethargic, slothful. The person can barely be animated to get anything done. One can talk to them about the bread of life and they are barely animated. What motivates them? What gets them going? Not that. Job's hope is contrasted with those attitudes.

Zophar: The Wicked

By the end of chapter 19 Job says, "Take heed of yourselves." This is Job's warning to these friends who are accusing him of vanity. He tells them, you'd better take heed for yourself if you don't know these things. Did Zophar listen to Job? No, he is troubled by all this. "My troubling thoughts prompted me to answer because I am greatly disturbed" (20:2). We might initially think that is good—Zophar is taking heed to himself. "I hear a rebuke that dishonors me and my understanding inspires me to reply" (v3). This is the last time we'll hear from Zohar—he does not show up in the next round. In this second and last time, he continues the formula from Eliphaz: only the wicked suffer. This formula is being imposed on Job and it does not fit. There is a kind of common sense operating in Zophar: you're suffering, therefore you're wicked. It is common sense. It looks round, therefore, it is round. Or, it looks flat, therefore it is flat. I had an argument once with the three-year-old who was on my shoulders. "Dad, is the earth flat?" No, it is like a sphere. It looks flat. Well, because we are little and on the surface of it, it kind of looks flat, but we are actually on the surface of a sphere. "No, it's flat, Dad. It looks flat." If that is what it looks like, I am asking this person to not believe their eyes. Believe me; don't believe what you immediately see in front of you. No—why? I am going to believe my eyes: it is flat.

Zophar is like that. You're wicked, Job. You're suffering. You've clearly sinned. How could this be otherwise? He ends in 20:29: "This is the fate that God allots all the wicked. It is the heritage appointed to them by God." His is a colorful speech; we can read through the kinds of things that befall the wicked. We can ask with Job, is this really what you see around you? We can do a simple look-out-the-window test. Is this what you see happening to the wicked when you look around you? And that is what Job says: can you listen carefully to my words? Listen to me.

We get the sense here that Job and the friends have not yet been talking with each other so much as at each other. That is why I said it is a dialogue, but it is also just speeches in a sense. We may have been in a situation where someone's talking at us...going on 45 minutes. It is not really a dialogue. Job asks in 21:3: Would you like someone to diligently listen to you? Job has been troubled by his friends' lack of pity. But his condition is due to the hand of God, so that is where he turns his complaint again. He once again turns to God, and he says, look, the wicked actually prosper in this life and the good suffer. That is what testimony of all humans will tell you when you ask them.

The Wicked Do Not Suffer

These three friends have hardened in their views and focused more narrowly on the plight of the wicked. But their theory does not actually hold up when Job looks at it. The wicked don't suffer. In 21:14, Job says, "They say to God, leave me alone." They don't want to have anything to do with God. And then they go on and they have a very good life. How often do we actually see the lamp of the wicked snuffed out vs. prospering? How often are they like straw before the wind? Psalm 1 addresses that. Is that really right? Are they like straw before the wind? Job's saying, no, it is not. I look around and they are doing very well for themselves. They steal from the poor, they build their houses, and they give to their children and go on. At least we can say, yes, but they still die. Well, Job addresses that. In 21:19, it says, "At least God stores up a man's punishment for his sons; let him repay the man himself so he may know about it." Does that knowledge comfort us at all? "At least Gilgamesh's children fell on hard times." Or should the wicked be punished for their own sins? Well, at least they all die. Worms cover them both. Yeah, well do you know what happens? The wicked have a wonderful life of prosperity, the righteous are tormented all the days of their lives, and they both become worm food. That is literally right there in 21:26. What was the purpose of striving and suffering? We can hear Asaph here. We wonder if Asaph maybe read Job when he wrote Psalm 73. What's the purpose of striving? You both become worm food, and the wicked have a much nicer life.

Job's view is hardening here. He is starting to say some things where we might wonder, well, wait a minute. But again, he is appealing to the common experience of humans. He even says, don't you talk to travelers? Those who have been to the far parts of the world will come to you here and they will tell you the same thing. It happens everywhere this way. He summarizes and ends it in 21:34: "How can you console me? How can you comfort me with your vanity? Nothing is left of your answers but falsehood." That "vanity" word is translated "nonsense." Nonsense is not comforting. And he has just soundly refuted their claims—they are false. There is no comfort in their words. But Job's view has also gotten harder. We are going to see where he goes in round three. There is no comfort in vanity.

Have the friends gotten any closer in this to overcoming their self-deception? Have they been able to examine their own views and assumptions? As I said, there is not much more for Zophar to go. So, he is done, ended in those ridiculous claims, not understanding what Job is going through in order to comfort his friend. They've hardened their views more narrowly based on a very thin sliver of understanding of what happens to the wicked in this life. Who will understand Job's case and plead for him, and who will be a witness for Job?

Where Is Comfort?

The second round hasn't given us satisfaction by itself. I have wanted to help us see how to get through Job as we enter the midst of Job, and how to think of the principles we need to have in place as the bread of life while we interpret our own experiences. But in terms of the arc of the narrative here, we are left without comfort. We have learned this pattern about how our inner thoughts are coming out in our times of suffering, and how they are tested, and that Job and his comforters are being exposed more and more. And Job has asked for comfort, for hope, for his words to be written down as a witness, and for a redeemer. Can we also, in our struggles, affirm what we know? When we are struggling, can we say, "I am suffering, but I know that my redeemer lives"? It is not limited there. We list what we do know: I am suffering and it is confusing, but I do know this. That is my rock. Remember, we are being written on the rock. Build on that rock. To do this, we have to be prepared ahead of time by coming to know these things.

So we can use this and put ourselves in the same situation to say, what do I know? What is my comfort? What is my condition before God? We don't want to use silly and simple formulas. Maybe we have gotten them from our personal experience. Maybe we have had a religious experience like Eliphaz did. But we haven't tested this in light of the word of God. Or we have relied on tradition. We are comfortable because we say, this is what the tradition teaches. I can be confident in that. Or we are good with common sense—I believe my eyes. And in doing this, we may misinterpret our own life and the lives of others.

So as we continue in this process with Job, we can use it as an opportunity to stop and think. Take heed of yourself, for judgment will come there as well. We should fear as well. Fear God. We think about this now as it applies to the Lord's Supper. We do have a redeemer. Our redeemer lives. How magnificent a truth that we get to remember. Remember Me. What divine glory is revealed in this? In Hebrews 5, we read of how Jesus is our priest, our mediator, an unending priesthood—what Job was looking for. We are on the other side of that event from Job, looking forward to it. We remember it now, and what our redeemer did for us, what he had to go through, including the mocking, like Job suffered. "He trusted in God; let him deliver him if he delights in him." And the mocking of Christ on the cross—our mediator. He offered up prayers. Hebrews 5 says, "He offered up prayers for us." Christ, our priest, praying for us. Job asked for a witness of what he was going through, and we see this in Christ. We read in Psalm 118, including verse 17: "I shall not die but live and tell the works of the Lord." Think of how that applies to David. It applies to us. As I continue to live, I go on to tell the works of the Lord. But also, this is the final psalm that Christ sang in The Last Supper, before they went out to the garden and he was arrested. So he is singing of himself, that he will not be given over the grave. I will not die, but live and tell the resurrection. I will see God in the flesh. I am thankful for this witness of our brother Job as he is gone through these. Our redeemer lives.

Job Part Four

Consider My Servant Job

23:2-4

Even today my complaint is bitter; his hand is heavy in spite of my groaning. If only I knew where to find him; if only I could go to his dwelling! I would state my case before him and fill my mouth with arguments.

We come now to the third and final round with Job's comforters. We continue with the problem that Job has presented us: Does any of this make sense? Can we understand? Is there any meaning? Any hope? Can we relate to those questions? We can relate to those questions—maybe the older you are, the more we relate; the more the syllogism begins to apply to us: all men are mortal, and Socrates is a man, therefore Socrates is mortal. That is all good when we are young, and then it starts to dawn on us: wait—that first premise said *all*. And we begin to think about how that means not just Socrates, but me. What's the meaning of it all? How can I understand this—not only that final sense of death, but also the trials that we go through in life? Why go through these?

Eliphaz: Job Is a Wicked Sinner

In chapter 22, Eliphaz gives the first response in this third round. It is his last for the book. What he says is that Job has sinned. He is pressed now by Job; there is a change in each of these responses. It is not just the same thing across the board. Each response requires the characters in the book to go deeper or harden in their position. Eliphaz has gone from some general claims about wicked people (although in those cases I showed how he actually says things about Job), and now he goes directly to: Job is a wicked person. He lists some things: Job has done the sins of oppression and injustice, of atheism and infidelity. And then he ends all that with some advice for Job. That is chapter 22. In 23 Job wrestles with what he just said and why his appeal is not being heard, and again asks, what is the meaning of the suffering he is going through? And in 24 Job continues this, and he is addressing this formula that they've had.

The formula is that the innocent do not suffer. Job gives some more examples of how that is just not true, that many of those who are innocent suffer, and there many who are wicked and don't get punished. Then chapter 25 is Bildad: his third and last interaction. It is very short. Bildad has been pushed. He was the one who appealed to tradition. In this interaction, he simply speaks of the infinite distance between God and man. Chapters 26-31 are all Job speaking. 26 is especially a reply to Bildad, and Job says, what you know, I also know. He said that before and he says it again here, about God and the wicked. And in 27, Job speaks of his own integrity, his dread of hypocrisy and of the wicked. In 28 he gives a story of those who seek the treasures of this world, ending with what we read: the fear of the Lord. That is easy to remember: Job 28:28 we can tattoo that on our mind. Then in chapter 29 Job describes his own view of his life, his prosperity and his hopes.

In chapter 30, we can focus on these two words: "but now." My hopes... But now... And we'll see what Job says about his miserable condition. Then in chapter 31 Job acquits himself of all of those accusations that have been made. He had asked for God to come down and speak with him, and at this point that hadn't happened, so he acquits himself; he takes that role on himself.

As we are going through these chapters, we need to keep in mind the biblical worldview. As I look at different commentaries, especially if they are from unbelievers, Job attracts everybody. It is almost a kind of general revelation book. And I look at commentaries or discussions of Job, and how people are shaped by the presuppositions they bring to the text. It is not a surprise. We are bringing the Biblical Worldview in Genesis 1-3 to these questions, and I made the case that Job could have known about God and our highest good from general revelation. And we are especially remembering the relationship between natural and moral evil and the difference between root sin and fruit sin. If we keep those differences in mind, then many of the accusations that are made about Job fall into place.

Those differences are not normally kept in mind; I don't know that I have found anybody in commentaries keeping that in mind about Job. Natural evil is not simply a call back from moral evil; it is the third call back from moral evil. It is imposed on the world by God in response to self-deception and self-justification. Because of those, we need natural evil—we are going to defend ourselves. I read a brief passage from Milton about what the demons in hell are doing. Of course, this is fictional, but it is a picture of even in that condition, where you might think you would wake up and repent, and instead, they are in deep deception and justification about their condition.

Have You Considered God's Servant Job?

This last round of replies and then in addition to it, Job's conclusion, is going to make us remember the title of the chapter from the beginning: Have you considered my servant Job? To whom was that question directed? Maybe we thought it was just directed to Satan. It certainly is directed at him in that context, but this is not only to him. *We* have the book. Have *we* considered God's servant Job? And you is "you," and it is the singular, but it is also the plural, and it is the plural of humanity. Have you considered God's servant Job? Why haven't we done this before? And what is seen here about Job? Because in this chapter, we have Job's concluding remarks. And especially when we are considering God's servant Job, these are what we would mainly focus on, having gone through the fiery trials he went through. But then what is worse? This interaction with these three comforters produces Job's conclusion. And we want to look at that conclusion.

The wisdom of patient Job: it is called a discourse in the Hebrew and it is translated "parable" in the authorized version. "Parable" makes us think mainly of stories. It is similar to the idea in a few of the Psalms, including Psalm 78 by Asaph—it means "instructions of the wise." Here we will be instructed by Job. We find his wisdom presented here for all to consider. Would we like to learn of the wise, the instructions of the wise? We will get those instructions from Job, and I saw how much I have missed in my reading of Job as I thought about them that way, and how much is there. Matthew Henry, one of the commentaries I use, said that, "We find here, in the Book of Job, the first and great principles of the light of nature on which natural religion is founded." Job is not quoting scripture; he is referring to and using the light of nature. And it is that on which we have natural religion.

Silenced

Chapter 22: the end of the discussion. The comforters are silenced. For those who wonder what silencing someone looks like, they can look to Job's discourse. How does he do that? I mean, Zophar does not even show up. He was done in round two with nothing more to say. This has been a discussion between persons who all affirm God and God's sovereignty. Job's comforters are pious. We could imagine a very different kind of discourse between Epicureans and Job. The Epicureans would say Job is a fool because he trusted God—of course there is no God. But the book of Job is not that. These are persons who profess to believe in God. And here they are, already at this early stage in history, with these divisions that have come up. And they are not able to agree. These most pious persons come to Job and they don't know themselves. What will the state of the world be if they don't know? If this is the condition of the time of the wise, and these are the best answers they've got? What are we going to expect in history after that? And supposing this is roughly the time of Abraham or maybe a little before, we'd see then the call of Abraham, and we'll have God's answer to that—what will happen. But here we have the Gentiles, the pious Gentiles, and they know a lot. We should quiz ourselves against them and see if we know as much as they do before we dismiss them.

Eliphaz: Job Is an Idolator

Here we have Eliphaz, the most sophisticated of the three. He is reduced to accusing Job of atheism and idolatry. He points out many true things. Both Eliphaz and Bildad in these sections point out things that are true and that we should take to heart. One of the problems, however, is that they are misapplied in the case of Job. Job is not an idolater. But we should avoid idolatry. So we don't need to dismiss Eliphaz—he is right about that. We should be pious.

He begins this way: God condescends to us. God is above us. Nothing we do or say profits God. The covenant God established with us is on God's part alone—it is God's graciousness towards us. That is true. Our invented religions are useless. We don't even live up to our own standards that we make. The New Year is when we make standards for ourselves. And then shortly after that is the time of year where we have already broken them and we have to start again. We can't live up to the standards we make for ourselves, let alone standards that God has set out for us. And then Eliphaz gets into the wickedness of humanity. He gives specific accusations. 22:5: "Is not thy wickedness great and thine iniquities infinite?"

This is not going to be merely him saying, "Hey, you're fallen; I am fallen; we're all fallen." He is going to get into some details now. What especially recurs in these chapters are the widow and the orphan—taking advantage of the weak. Those are two examples of the weak in this condition. I think we could see how they have that general characteristic, but also apply it in our situation. Who is the weak in our situation? In 22:9: "Thou hast sent widows away empty and the arms of the fatherless have been broken." We are told true religion is to care for orphans and widows. That is in the New Testament. Here we have in the Old Testament the same theme. Eliphaz says Job is not even doing the basics of religion. You don't care for orphans and widows, Job. You turn them away empty.

And then in 22:12 we get into what I am going to call biblical atheism. Is that a good term? Hey, there is biblical atheism. It is sanctioned by the Bible. Well, it is the kind of atheism the Bible talks about. For example, in Psalm 14, it is the fool who said there is no God. And the biblical atheist is not merely the Epicurean who says only atoms and the void exist. The biblical atheist is the contemporary materialist. That person is sort of the easy one. Even Epicurus himself speaks at times as if there is a God; he just does not do anything. That is closer to it. Biblical atheism is laid out in 22:12: "Is not God in the heights of heaven and behold, the height of the stars, how high they are. And thou sayest, what does God know? Can he judge through the dark cloud?" God exists and he does not do anything. That is atheism. And Eliphaz charges Job with this. If we think about that, it is very similar to what starts to occur in Babylon, in Babel, and their view of the gods and the high God. God is up there in his heaven, and all is well with the world. It is quite the opposite. God is in his heaven and nothing is well with the world.

So, we have to take it in our own hands to make something better with the world—atheistic humanism. We'll have to build our own towers to the heavens. In

22:15, Eliphaz says this of Job: "Hast thou marked the old way which wicked men have trodden, which were cut down out of time, whose foundation was overflown with a flood?" Is Job like those ancient and wicked people who had to be destroyed by a flood? Now we can play with that; this is the Flood. And we could play with some other alternatives; no, it is just *a* flood; there is some other flood that overthrew wicked people that is not recorded in scripture. Overthrown by the Flood. Eliphaz is calling Job the same as the ancient atheists—Job of all people—in order to justify himself. Here's what they said to God: "Depart from us. What can the Almighty do to us?" That was their atheism, Biblical atheism.

Then, in 22:20, it gets worse—if it possibly could. Look who he is about to call Job. "Whereas our substance is not cut down, but the remnant of them the fire consumeth." Who is this "remnant" of the wicked pre-flood persons that were consumed by fire? Those were the sodomites continuing that ancient heresy—the remnant of them, that ancient belief. He is calling Job one of those who are consumed by the fire! One might say there are other stories of people being consumed by fire that aren't recorded in scripture. But I think this is talking about that event. He is accusing Job even of that.

Repent

These are the accusations; this is the place it has gotten to. However, Eliphaz says, I have some advice for you. "If thou return to the Almighty, thou shalt be built up, thou shalt put away iniquity far from thy tabernacles." (22:23). Just repent, return to God, and all will be well with you. For then shalt thou have thy delight in the Almighty, and shalt lift up thy face unto God" (22:25). That is good advice. Do it. We should not think that since this advice is from Eliphaz, it is bad advice that we should not do. We should find our comfort and delight in God. But think of the discourse before that. This is a problem. Eliphaz hasn't gotten to his root sin. He is at the point where he is frustrated with Job and he is making these accusations which seem quite wild. "Make your prayer unto him and he shall hear you and you shall pay your vows." And then: "When men are cast down, then you shall say, there is lifting up, and he will save the humble person." You'll be in a situation where you can help others later. And that does happen. A person may go through a kind of a trial, and then they can help others through a very similar trial. That does happen, although it can be circular if we don't understand the purpose of it. Why do I suffer? So that you can help other people who suffer. Well, why are they suffering? So that later on they are able to help other people who suffer. So, there must be more to it than that.

Job: Where Is God?

In chapter 23, in response to this problem of suffering of the just, Eliphaz says God must be just. Job wants God to hear his complaint, which presumes God is just, so by implication Job affirms the justice of God. Where is God? he asks. And especially in 23:5: "I would know the words which he would answer me and understand what he would say to me." Job is redirecting. He is continuing to bring back his accusers to that point. He is not going to let go of these awful accusations, but he does not let himself get distracted by them. He wants to understand why and he hasn't yet been told why. And in verse 7, he wants deliverance, even from his judge. Deliverance in this life. There is the idea that at death everyone's sorted out—but what about in this life? Do we just have to wait till death, and then the wicked get what's coming to them? Or is there deliverance in this life? What is the meaning and the purpose of it? That is verse 8: "Behold, I go forward, but he is not there, and backward, but I cannot perceive him." Job does not understand. Where is God? And we'll get this interesting thing in Job here in these couple chapters: God is right there and I don't get it, I don't perceive him. And in other chapters, he will say, I don't know where he is. He is absent. There is a confusion in Job. He says: the foot of justice is on me. I don't understand—or, God is absent; I have cried and asked for help. Where is God? And in 23:10: "But he knoweth the way that I take; when he hath tried me, I shall come forth as gold."

This is the sense of suffering Job has. He knows that from this fiery trial, gold is produced; there is a reference here to that, how gold is refined. It is called, sometimes, the purgative role of suffering. Purgation is the burning away of remaining error. So, he affirms that here. And we can affirm that in general with Job; the problem is to get into the details of it. How does it work out for us? How does this work out for me? And now we have these accusations. In 23:13: "Does God deal unaccountably? But he is of one mind, and who can turn to him? And what his soul desireth, even that he doeth." In the NIV, it says, "But he stands alone, and who can oppose him?" He does whatever he wants. God does whatever he wants. It seems inexplicable. Why is this happening the way it is? And then in verse 15: "Therefore, I am troubled at his presence." But before he was saying, I have asked for his presence and he won't speak to me. "I am troubled by his presence when I consider I am afraid of him." Verse 16: "He troubleth me."

Here is some of this wrestling of Job. And I would suspect we have wrestled in a similar way. Chapter 24 has the ends of the wicked. "Why, seeing times are not hidden from the Almighty, do they that know him not see his days?" And then he gives a list of some of the kinds of evils that persons do and how they come to nothing. Social evils. And people ask, where is God in all of this? This is the counterfactual response. There are people who do these wicked things and bad things don't seem to happen to them. Job again gets into some of the same problems: oppressing the weak, the fatherless and the widow or oppressed. They move landmarks, they lie about who owns what land. In 24:9: "They pluck the fatherless from the breast and take a pledge of the poor." And in 24:12: "Where is God? Men groan. The soul of the wounded cries out. Yet God layeth not folly to them."

Eliphaz gave us that formula from the very beginning, and Job has just been giving simple counterfactuals. It makes you wonder about these three guys. Do they observe anything in the world? Sometimes that happens, people don't observe but they have this formula they work with. And remember, for Eliphaz, it came to him in a dream. He had what he considered a kind of special revelation where he is told this in a dream. It has solidified his whole outlook on life. "The innocent don't suffer." What? Just open the door and look outside! And Job's doing that with him, thinking through that process. That is part of the silencing, taking this thought captive. There is nothing more to say to defend that formula. Chapter 24:13: "They are those that rebel against the light. They know not the ways thereof nor abide in the paths thereof." Job talks about a murderer, a thief who goes in to steal and murders the person. That happens. It is an awful thing. And God does not do anything about that, does he? The guy gets away. Murders unsolved. Watching those forensic files—sometimes there are unsolved ones. The cops can get the murderers usually. But if they are careful, sometimes they can get away with the murder.

Or how about in 24:15: The adulterer who goes in and destroys a family and gets away with it. He searches his own pleasure and then gets away with it. And so, we wonder where God is—and where is justice? In verse 24 it says, "They are exalted for a little while, but are gone and brought low. They are taken out of the way as all others and cut off as the tops of the ears of corn." All others. That is part of the problem. The guy who's the adulterer, the murderous thief—they end up dead, and so does everyone else who did not do that. So, the lesson, I guess? Just do it. Just go ahead and do evil.

Job gives a challenge at the end of that chapter: "And if this be not so now, who will make me a liar, make my speech nothing worth?" (v25). Silence me. If this does not happen, show me that it does not happen. The wise and the fool, the wicked and the innocent—all end up dead, roughly in the same way. Where is this formula you're working with? Eliphaz is done. Job gives a challenge; there is no response to that.

Bildad: How Can We Be Justified?

Chapter 25 gives us Bildad's final speech and the end of the replies of the friends. He can be summarized as telling us to remember our condition. What's the application of this? He says of God, "Dominion and fear are with him. He maketh peace in his high places. Is there any number of his armies and upon whom doth not his light arise? How, then, can man be justified with God? Or how can he be clean that is born of a woman?" (v2-4) So we are all fallen, God is infinite, God is above all things. What's the application? Or are these just more platitudes? Bildad's tradition, his appeal to what the fathers before us have taught, is reduced to just some platitudes. How does this help me understand my situation? Why exactly is this happening to me? What is the meaning of it?

Job: What You Know I Know

Job answers Bildad in chapter 26 with a theme he is used before: what you know, I know. I won't go into it, but there is much silliness that comes up in historical textual criticism about these next chapters. These are all Job speaking, but since Zophar does not show up, people raise some questions like, maybe one of these got misnamed and it is really Zophar. No. I think we can understand how all these are Job, and how they fit perfectly in place. Because Job starts to say some things here which seem to go against what he said earlier. But what he is doing is this: he knows the formula these guys used. He understands the innocent don't suffer and the wicked do suffer. He understands it even better than they do. He ends up basically showing them: I know your view better than you know it, even after having falsified it. I know what you know. What good has come? Job says this in 26:3: "How hast thou counseled him that hath no wisdom? And how hast thou plentifully declared the thing as it is?" What good has come of anything that his comforters have said? They haven't been able to defend themselves, their own view, instruct Job, or help anyone listening. Nothing good has come of their view. They haven't instructed anybody. And we all have to take that to heart and think before we speak.

Job has wisdom also. And he gives an example now of his wisdom about these matters. So he is answering them. There are two ways to answer them: according to what they are saying, and then also to silence them. Job does both here, and in the rest of this chapter he goes through the list of all the ways in which God's providence works. Starting in 26:5: "The dead are in deep anguish, those beneath the waters and all that live in them. Death is naked before God, destruction lies uncovered. He spreads out the northern skies over empty space, he suspends the earth over nothing." So, he goes through a list here of God's sovereignty as creator. And think about this; we come later to what God says. How is this any different than what God says later? Does Job already know that? And each of these is worth reflecting on.

Just think about this one: he suspends the earth over nothing. If someone has ever tried to hang a picture, they would know how hard it is. I was told once that I hung a picture crooked. It required two nails, and I stepped back and it was crooked. It is fine, it'll be good enough. No, it is driving me crazy. It is crooked. I have to straighten it. I can't even hang a picture on a wall with a hammer and nails, let alone hang the earth on nothing. Look at the infinite power of God to hang the world in space like that. Job goes through a list: by his Spirit, he is garnished the heavens; his hand has formed the crooked serpent.

He is beginning now to answer them. In chapter 25, we had Bildad; in 26 Job answers him, and then in 27 we begin to get into this discourse of Job, a parable, the instruction of the wise. And this is where I say, consider God's servant Job. And because of reading this and because of reading those words of Matthew Henry earlier, Job's role as a philosopher dawned on me. Job sets aside his sores and does philosophy.

I have told people that philosophy began with this fellow who said all is water, and I talked about Socrates as being a kind of father-like figure to the philosophers. I need to rethink that and think of Job's role here in human history so early, as a Gentile, doing philosophy, and how he does it, and contrast it with those biblical atheists, two of which I just mentioned (whether you go the direction of the materialist or the direction of saying God may exist, but he is not active and involved in the world). We get Job's instructions on wisdom. And like Job's comforters, all we can do is sit back in silence and read these and reflect on them.

The Hypocrite

Job speaks especially in chapter 27 of the hypocrite, his enemy. 27:7: "Let mine enemy be as the wicked; he that rises up against me as the unrighteous. For what is the hope of the hypocrite though he hath gained, when God taketh away his soul?" And we know those words of Christ against the hypocrite. That is a standard problem. The hypocrite is a standard character in the biblical story; hence it is one that we should pay attention to and avoid. We might think about how easy it is not to go into someone's house and murder them while we are stealing their stuff. It is pretty easy not to do that, I guess. I would think it would take some planning to do it. But being a hypocrite may sneak up on us. Self-deception and self-justification. And we may especially think of ourselves as very pious. The hypocrites did think that way of themselves. They aren't the materialists. There might be something refreshing about the Epicurean who just says plainly, look, it is all matter. As opposed to the hypocrite: brood of vipers, trying to be secretive, trying to be deceptive, especially fooling the simple. So, the hypocrite is here and in verses 7-10. And then Job says in 11, "I will teach you by the hand of God; that which is with the Almighty will I not conceal." This continues that theme I just mentioned of "I know what you knew, or what you claim to know, as well."

Job gets into a discourse by the end about the wicked, which sounds somewhat like his comforters. But again, I think this is the strategy that he is working with: those that remain of the wicked shall be buried in death, and his widow shall not weep. And he goes over a list of very awful things that come upon the wicked. "Though he heap up silver as the dust to prepare raiment as the clay. He may prepare it, but the just shall put it on and the innocent shall divide the silver." Job's affirming that he is not in the situation of saying the wicked life is a good way of life. He affirms here that this leads to destruction. Ultimately, the just do prevail. But that does not help us with the counterfactuals that he considered, the counterfactuals being the contrast with that argument. We go outside and see suffering. To simply affirm that the wicked come to a bad end and the just rule doesn't help us with that. But here he affirms that of course he knows that. "Don't I know that as well?" Don't I also know that God is good and God is just, and the path of the wicked leads to destruction? So again, it is this question: what were you comforters exactly instructing me about? I know those things as well as you do.

Job's Parable

In chapter 28, Job gets into a story. This is like a parable, and it should remind us of the parable of the pearl of great price or the hidden treasure. Think of what people go through to search for gold. And this is where I put this up against Socrates. Tell me who is the philosopher, because of where they come out. Put this up against Thales, and tell me who was doing philosophy. How should philosophy be done and how should it be taught? And this is from the light of nature and those eternal truths of natural religion, which is to say it could be taught in the secular sphere. It is not an appeal to revealed religion.

Think of what men do to find gold. There is some interesting descriptions here of how they were mining back then, and all that they go through to get gold or silver, or the places they go to get sapphires. Early mining. We think of it now as sort of a dangerous profession; it sounded even more dangerous then. Not to mention the coral or the pearls, right? Job talks here about going into the earth, into cracks in the earth, to find these things. I was out hiking and came across a mine shaft, probably about 40 feet down, just straight down. There was a pile of the rubble that they brought up out of the mine shaft. It probably just had a rope and a pulley and a bucket. Shoveling rocks in this bucket and the guy up on top pulls it up. Keep going, looking for something that you can sell, something of value. Not to mention, how do you get coral or pearls? How long can you hold your breath? There are guys who can hold their breath for 15 minutes or something. Can we dive down there and get what treasures the bottom of the ocean has to offer? Think of the effort in both cases that is being exerted. And now think about wisdom. 28:20: "Whence then cometh wisdom, and where is the place of understanding?"

It is interesting that understanding did factor in, because we need understanding to get these things out of the earth. Where is understanding coming from? To what extent do we pursue wisdom? And so, we are reminded of the parable, the pearl of great price. Here we have Job at the very beginning of these thoughts in human history, asking the same question. What do we do to get wisdom? And he affirms here something of God's secret or hidden will, and man and his revealed will in 28:20, "Whence cometh wisdom and where is a place of understanding, seeing it is hid from the eyes of all living and cut close from the fowls of the air? Destruction and death themselves say they've only heard of it. God understands the way thereof and he knows the place thereof."

So, the summary of Job, as a philosopher: behold, the fear of the Lord, that is wisdom, and to depart from evil is understanding. It is such an early time in human history and he is already affirming this. Philosophy should get us there because of the very name of it. Do we love wisdom? Then we'd pursue it like this and we would not end up in biblical atheism, affirming some kind of demiurge or first cause who is no longer acting in the world. The summary of Job's teaching. Have you considered God's servant Job?

But Now . . .

Job continues in this parable in chapter 29, and there are similar ones in Psalms 142, 148, and 78. 29 is a beautiful chapter. "Oh, that I were as in months past, as in the days when God preserved me" (v2). When I was in my prime. Job's ideal life. It is something like reflecting on the golden days. Do we remember those days? Make my life great again. And we reflect back on when it was so good and sweet. It is something of the fantasy life. Because some of this may not have actually been as good as we thought it was, and especially when we project it into the future. Sometimes we call it the self-life, but at the same time, those might give something of a ring of sin. I think what Job is talking about here are very natural things to want. In the days of my youth, my prime. And here is how it is phrased in verse 6: "When I washed my steps with butter and the rock poured me out rivers of oil." Can we imagine the abundance? All that we could want, the best things in life, so much of them that it is pouring out.

And Job had respect. Remember in the beginning of the book when he had respect? Would we like to have respect? Does it get to us when we are not respected, like if we are walking to the kitchen and someone comes past us and they do something that seems like a disrespectful gesture? But then we are not sure and spend the rest of the day thinking about it—I think that person disrespected me. I demand respect. We might get to a point where we just make it humorous and say, "I get no respect." But Job says in 29:8: "The young men saw me and hid themselves, and the aged arose and stood up." The young and the old, respectively. He is remembering that time. Incidentally, in verse 5, he says, "When the Almighty was yet with me and when my children were with me." That is what gets to me—think of Job's children, dead. He remembers that. What's more natural than wanting that, to be with your family? To have them gathered around at that time of year. There is no place like home at Christmas time, and everyone is there. And Job was respected. The old and the young respected him. He says in verse 12: "I delivered the poor that cried out, the fatherless, and him that had none." I helped him. I caused the widow's heart to sing for joy.

He begins to get into these denials of what he is been accused of. "I said, 'I shall die in my nest and I shall multiply my days as the sand'" (29:18). We have that vision of our future, dying in our nest with our kids around us—a happy ending after a happy life. And that is what Job expected out of life. So, we have chapter 28, what do we do to seek wisdom, and chapter 29, the natural view of what we want of life. And Job had gotten that, hadn't he? He had his children around him, he had wealth—so that he is using butter to wash his steps. He had all those things. This is what we expect out of life. We may call it the prosperity gospel—he had named it and claimed it. And then one can look forward and say: and then I'll just die in my happiness; I'll die in this contentment. It is almost a way of downplaying death, and it should not ever be downplayed. Even if you have all that stuff, death is awful. Why do I have to die in the first place? But it is a way of mitigating it and minimizing it. I've got all these things, I have my kids and my family around me, and then in that situation I'll go on to the next life. It is the best possible way to die. "My glory was fresh in me; my bow was renewed in my hand"(29:20). Verse 25: "I chose out their way and sat as chief and dwelt as king in the army, as one that comforteth the mourners."

Job had a prime position in society. In chapter 30, he says, "But now." What actually happened? What hurt him the most? Turn to chapter 30 to find out. Does he give us a medical history of his sores? Does he say, on my arm here, I have a white discoloration. What is that? What hurt him the most? He describes here: the loss of that respect. This is what hurt worse than the sores.

Chapter 30:1: "But now, they who are younger than I have me in derision, whose fathers I would have disdained to have set with the dogs of my flocks." A young man who is from a notable family mocks Job. How much more so everyone else? "But now." What a turnaround. And that is what Job describes first: how others held him in contempt. He goes on and discusses this in other details. "They abhor me. They flee far from me and spare not to spit in my face." We can anticipate it even if we haven't been there—going through that trial and seeing even those who were closest to us turn their backs on us and spit in our face. Those who had said they were our friends. When the suffering comes, where are those who said they were friends?

This culminates in the chief example: "He who broke bread with me has lifted up his heel"(Psalm 41:9). Judas Iscariot. The betrayer. There are many instances like that of Job foreshadowing the suffering of Christ. But we can relate to it as well. And that is what Job mentions here, as opposed to, "I had all these camels they took. These were nice camels." I mean, have you ever appreciated a camel? Let me tell you about the camel. Job could go into that, but he doesn't. He goes into this (30:16): "And now my soul is poured out upon me; the days of affliction have taken hold upon me." Life is ebbing away from Job. He is not going to have that end he wanted. How does someone get their kids back? We can get back our stuff, but we won't have that end we'd envisioned.

Will it all work out in the end? Even if it does that does not explain why it had to be this way. Where was God? Verse 20: "I cry unto Thee and Thou does not hear me; I stand up and thou regardest me not. Thou art become cruel to me; with Thy strong hand Thou opposed thyself against me." Job had said, "I will not abandon my integrity." And now he gets into accusing God. This is what's going to cause some of the problems that Job encounters. He gets into a dangerous position now. But he is still affirming again the sovereignty of God. God is sovereign in all these things. But where is God? How do we make sense of it in light of how we understand God? He responds to this claim he did not help others in verse 25: "Did I not weep for him that was in trouble? Was not my soul grieved for the poor?"

I Am Innocent

Then in chapter 31 Job acquits himself of all the accusations that have just been made. He had asked God to give him a trial so he could state his case. And as he just said, where is God? I have heard nothing, so now I'll acquit myself. I'll defend myself. And it is about the things that Eliphaz had said—but does Job get to root sin? If he gets past this he could repent at a deeper level. And so, in verse 31, he talks about lust of the eyes. "I did not give in to the lust of the eyes." It is not simply that I did not commit adultery with my neighbor's wife. That is a low mark, right? I haven't done that. "I made a covenant with my eyes not to look at a maiden." That is a much higher mark, and that is what he did. "For what portion of God is there from above, and what inheritance of the Almighty from on high? Is not destruction to the wicked and a strange punishment to the workers of iniquity?" And then he gives some "ifs" in this chapter. 31:5: "If I have walked in vanity, or if my foot has haste to deceit, let me be weighed in an even balance, that God may know my integrity." Job goes through a number of these. He is not merely saying "I am innocent"; he is saying, I did not do this, and if I did, let this occur to me. Let there be this consequence. And he says, I'll be willing to suffer the consequences if I had done these things. But I haven't done these things. If my steps had turned out of the way, then let me sow and another eat. If my heart had been deceived by a woman, then let my wife grind another man's grain (v9-10). If I despise a cause of the manservant or maidservant, then what shall I do when God rises up? (v13-14).

He goes through a number of these, almost like oaths. If I have done this, then let this occur to me. And it is interesting that in 31:15, he has a statement of equality. Why didn't he do these things? He gives a picture into his thinking. What can he know? Can he know moral law 5? Verse 15: "Did not he that made me in the womb make him?" He is talking about his servants. "And did not the One fashion us both?" He has this understanding in thinking about the equality of human nature: both made by God, both made in the image of God. That is why he did not do these things. And then he talks about how he did not oppress the fatherless, the orphan, in verse 17. In verse 21, again, the fatherless. He did not give in to avarice, in verse 24, or put his hope in gold. Hope is one of the things he is been asking—how do I get hope? And he did not find it in gold. He appeals to God the Creator as the basis for equality.

I Do Not Worship the Moon

And then it gets interesting in 31:26. I think this is in response to the claim of biblical atheism, but also it shows us some of the creeping in of idolatry in that ancient world. How would that have looked? "If I beheld the sun when it shined or the moon walking in brightness, and my heart had been secretly enticed or my mouth had kissed my hand." This apparently was a kind of ritual. You can't kiss the sun or the moon, they are so high above you, so you kiss your hand and point to the sun. I love the sun. It is the hottest place on earth (joke). And the moonites will say, no, don't overlook the moon. Where are you going to be without tides? Do you want to try living without tides? So, then, there is a civil war going between the moon and the sun worshipers. And we know these were springing up at the time. People worshiped these in Ur, and Abraham left. Nineveh was a city devoted to the moon goddess, all the way through history to the work of the Apostle Paul in the city of Ephesus, where they had this great silver statue of Diana. Then to the Americans who make movies about her still. Job says, I did not do these things. I suppose the polytheist think that behind the moon and the sun is the initial God. They are not saying there is only the sun; there is this god who made those things, but now the sun and moon rule us and we have got to worship them. Job says, I did not do that. He is not that kind of biblical atheist. Then, in 31:33, he says "If I had covered my transgressions as Adam, by holding my iniquity in my bosom..." Job is getting here to self-deception and self-justification. He did not cover himself as Adam did if he had done these things wrong.

Adam

Job goes back to the beginning. Eliphaz goes the flood; Job goes back to the very first thing. He says, I did not do what Adam did. In 31:35 he cries: "Oh, that one would hear me. Behold, my desire is that the Almighty would answer me, and that mine adversary had written a book." Well, we are about to get an answer, and there is a book: the book of Job. Have we considered God's faithful servant Job? Job says, "Surely I would take it upon my shoulder and bind it as a crown to me." I wonder, what would Job think of the book of Job now? "I would declare to him the number of my steps; as a prince would I go near unto him." And then in verses 38-40, he gives a final decree, an "if-then." "If my land cry against me or the furrows likewise thereof complain, if I have eaten the fruits thereof without money or have caused the owners thereof to lose their life, let thistles grow instead of wheat, and cockle instead of barley." Let my life come to nothing; let it bear no fruit. Not only let it bear no fruit, but let it bear thorns. This is also what was said of Adam: by the sweat of your brow you will work, and thorns will grow up. Your whole life comes to this; there will be no fruit from your life. This contrasts with what Job had said about what he expected out of life: to die with his fruit gathered around him. Is not that a sweet death, with all one's fruit there? Job says, no, if I have done what you've said, then let my life end like this. Then we have verse 40: "The words of Job are ended." We do not hear any more discourse from Job or these others—I think they've been silenced. But who is able to look on Job and understand what he is been going through? The last section there was the instructions of the wise. The instructions of wisdom are ended, and there is much to mine in those as we pursue wisdom.

The End of the Discourses

The Book of Job itself is not done. We have more to go. We are ending the discourses—we are ending the three rounds with his friends and seeing the ins and outs of that. And now we come to Elihu, and then God. But have we considered God's servant Job? Patient Job? Wise Job? And have we thought about what to expect in our life? We have all either gone through trials and tried to make sense of them, or, if we are on the younger side of the spectrum, what do we expect? Do we project forward the way Job did, and say, "Oh, I expected a delightful life"?

This book shows what we should expect and get an example of what we should be willing to go through and how we should be going through it. That is why 1 Peter 5:6-7 says, "Humble yourselves, therefore, under the mighty hand of God, that he may exalt you in due time, casting all your care upon him, for he careth for you." That is when Job begins to doubt. Does God care for me in this situation? Isn't this suffering the opposite of caring? If this is God's caring, I could use less of God's caring. God cares for us. Do we believe that? We can think of Peter's life and what it took for Peter to come to that point and what he went through. Humble yourself under the mighty hand of God, for he cares about you.

Job Part Five

Elihu Preparing the Way

33:8-9

But you have said in my hearing—I heard the very words—'I am pure, I have done no wrong; I am clean and free from sin'.

37:14

Listen to this, Job; stop and consider God's wonders.

What Will It Take?

We continue now with Elihu. What do we think about Elihu? He is a human and he is going to present us with an argument that prepares the way for God to speak. There is a seamless move from Elihu to God speaking. Elihu is not reprimanded with the other friends. We will evaluate him here on those terms. Consider his argument.

Is he going to help Job come to understand? Job has finished and his three friends are silenced. We do not yet have an answer to the question that we started with: how can our suffering make sense? Remember, Job put his emphasis on meaning. How can this trial have meaning? It might be interesting to see what level of suffering brings out that question in a person, because we see where it was for Job. And if we hear people complaining about their suffering, we might find out what it is. "Oh, that's it? That's all it took to make you cry out?" Or, "Wow, that's a lot." And we have seen what it took for Job. How do we make sense of this? Job's three comforters have failed to bring comfort, but Job has also failed to find meaning. He can't put the blame on them; he has a mind as well. What has happened in the dialogue portion is not just a hardening of a line. The lines were hardened, but the positions were also developed in greater consistency.

What was in Job has been drawn out for all of us to see. What will it take to get a person to seek God diligently? We can reflect on that for ourselves or others. We might start off with the assumption, well, I already am seeking God diligently, which means we are at the beginning of the story of Job.

What will it take? Here we are starting to see some of that. In Hebrews we are told that to please God, we must seek him diligently, believe that he is, and that he is the rewarder of those who diligently seek him. So we are going to see that with Job, and we are into that part of the book now. If we were to end the book now, it would be sort of a crushing defeat. Job responded to his friends, showing them he, too, knows what they say. He, too, knows that the wicked seem to get away with things in this life. And it is precisely because of where he ends that he is going to be reprimanded by Elihu.

So Elihu must prepare the way of the Lord. He is in a position not dissimilar to John the Baptist. Elihu gives his discourse, then there is no pause, no interruption, and God speaks. Elihu must prepare the way. And how is he going to do that? If we were in the place of Elihu, what would our witness be like to someone like Job? I said that Job really should replace Socrates as the father of philosophy, both because of the time (he is before Socrates) and because of the content. Socrates just does not get to where it needs to go; Job does. And really, Elihu is the one who gets there. These six chapters are incredibly profound in their insights. And perhaps because I have studied philosophy, a number of the issues stood out to me as I read commentaries of persons who hadn't studied philosophy. I was surprised at what they overlooked; surprised at the incomplete or even mistaken conclusions they drew.

Youth and Wisdom

Elihu is the youngest of the group and I want to look at how he presents himself. It is not what we would expect. We expect the sign in reality to be old age, gray hair, and wisdom. And we should have reverence for the old because of that normal connection. But what about when it does not happen? The youth are often quick to say wisdom not there in the aged when it is. So, they have to temper themselves. Elihu did that. We expect age and wisdom together. But this book challenges some of our beliefs about appearance and reality, including that one. We do not want just appearance; we want to get to reality. And these three comforters and Job, all older, haven't come to wisdom. How frustrating, because of the seriousness of the matter.

This is not a conference paper at a nice conference where you get some coffee and a biscuit and give your paper and everyone discusses abstract ideas. Look at what Job's going through. This is the real kind of research. It should focus our minds because Job went through it—remember, he said he wanted his words written down, and indeed they were. Would we like that to be written down about us? When all of our deepest thoughts come out, would we like the whole world to read them? I do not know that I would. Job's had that happen. All of his deepest thoughts have come out and they've been written down for the whole world to see. Consider my servant Job. Never overlook Job.

Elihu's Argument

Elihu is a human. He is not reprimanded at the end by God as the other three are. We will treat him as a human who is presenting an argument. Let's follow Elihu's thoughts, his argument, as we are going, and see what is it that makes him wise. We must begin with what we know about God. That is the structure of Elihu's thought, of his argument. He begins with the basics, the elementary truths. Here it is: we start with what we know about God. We don't doubt that. I'll show you how he does that in his argument. This includes God's nature and God's purpose. And if we kept that in mind, the whole structure of the book would have been different. That is the biblical worldview which is there from the beginning. I was charged recently by an atheist for imposing Christian ideas on the book of Job, and that instead, I should read it as a good secular humanist. Well, there is something to that. I do not want to impose ideas on a book.

But at the same time, this is in the Bible, it is part of the biblical worldview, and so we are going to assume the things that we can know. The eternal power and divine nature of God are clear from general revelation, the eternal power and divine nature, and Elihu's going to call our attention back to that. Had we kept this in mind, this whole dialogue between Job and his friends would have been different. God mercifully teaches us about ourselves. The part that I see overlooked in all, even the best-intentioned commentaries, is that God is long-suffering in teaching us about those things, including our self-deception and our self-justification. This is what's taking up so much time in history and personal interactions, since the very beginning. Why are you hiding, Adam? Why are you in self-deception? Why are you in self-justification? It wasn't me, it was her. Don't blame me; the devil made me do it. And think of how much time it takes to get through self-deception and deal with people.

Teachers sort of have this idea that they can teach. And in any job where one interacts with people, the assumption is, I have something to teach other people. A young person going into teaching—there is something a little bit prideful there. And in many cases, they may not. But they go into it quite energetically, quite excited. And then there is a burnout period, about five or six years in—the same as the marriage burnout period. The teacher gets into that and usually blames the students. The students are too difficult. They don't learn. I quit. And they stop teaching, they get a new job—I am out of here and on to a more enjoyable thing. And they are right...and they are wrong. I like to hold contradictions together in my mind. The teacher is right: the students are difficult to teach; but they haven't correctly diagnosed the problem. The students aren't simply blockheads; they are chips off the old block. The old block is Adam. And the students are in self-deception about their condition, and in self-justification, and only God is the model teacher.

That is the word Elihu actually uses here. God is long-suffering. And it is not merely that he will be long-suffering and keep repeating the ABCs to them over and over. Look at how God's going to use his long-suffering to get through their self-deception. It is not someone simply repeating themsleves again and again on the same topic without change. This is teleological. This is goal oriented. God is moving Job to get to know what he should know even in the face of self-deception and self-justification.

I do not see people drawing attention to that reality of human sin, root sin. Root sin plus self-deception and self-justification: that is the reality we are being exposed to here in Job. I don't see commentaries drawing attention to that. They might at best draw attention to God as a teacher. They might say that Job sinned, but they do not get to sin as inexcusable unbelief, as a failure to see what is clear from general revelation.

Whenever I read commentaries—the better ones—when I get to the chapters with Elihu or God, it is about how God is very powerful and we should just submit to his power. That is just what Job's friends had already told him, so it would not make any sense if that is the conclusion. Eliphaz says that, then God says the same thing, and then we are all done. That can't be it. No, there is a cover-up going on. Exposing cover-ups is exciting, isn't it? We follow the detective through people covering it up, and get back to the real cover-up. It was Sparky the Sun Devil the whole time, covering everything up! He has such an innocent-looking face, but he is diabolical.

We are going to get beyond these three rounds of not thinking. These three friends really had no ability to think critically about their own views. We just saw them harden. It should be a lesson to us. Can Elihu help us?

Do not Dismiss Elihu

A few words about those who dismiss Elihu. How has Elihu been interpreted? Here are five ways. Some people say there is a difference in chapter 32 where he is initially presented and then how he presents himself: that he is an arrogant young man. So, it shows a sort of lack of self-understanding on his part. Second, they say he is impetuous and filled with anger or wrath. Third, he describes himself as a windbag. He uses the same Hebrew term that Eliphaz earlier had used for being filled with gas in a negative sense—to be a fool. A windbag is a fool. Since he used that same phrase that Eliphaz used, some authors say, look, he is a self-described fool. Fourth, they say he takes God's side. He is not impartial to Job. He does more of the same: God is just, God rules, God can do whatever he wants; don't question him. And five, he continues the same type of argument that the friends had eventually ended in, which is accusing Job of sin. I defended Job in those portions against what they said. So now, how can I think Elihu is right?

My response to those five ways will come out in the text. We are going to evaluate Elihu in light of his argument, and see that he is preparing the way for what God is going to say in the next chapters. He is preparing the way of the Lord here. What is God going to say? As Elihu gets towards the end of his dialogue, he is beginning to do exactly what God then does with Job. Elihu reprimands Job for having justified himself and not God.

Consider the Argument

Man is a rational creature and can think and speak. We are going to consider Elihu on those terms, in terms of his argument. I don't know that there is anything wrong at all with his frustration. In fact, what I see modeled in the beginning of chapter 32 is that he says he remained silent—and indeed he does.

Some people think this section is just a later scribe's edition, because all of a sudden, here's Elihu, never mentioned, who did not say anything at all, then all of the sudden he speaks. Well, it is described here that he is held his tongue because he wants to listen to the older, supposedly wiser persons. And their dialogue has gotten to a natural ending. He is not interjecting in the middle of something; it ended naturally, and now he is going to say, "Here's what I think."

Elihu is angry because of how the friends and Job behaved themselves. We want to look at that reply and see how he is using rhetoric—again, we can go to Elihu as opposed to Aristotle as an example of how he speaks to Job and the friends to move them along. How does he silence his opponents and call them to repentance? That is masterful. And Elihu presents himself as young; he is willing to wait and listen, and he is speaking only when he sees that these others have failed.

The aged did not have wisdom, although that is a natural expectation. And that should make us angry. What normally makes us angry? Someone gets in our way in traffic? Things do not go our way and we generally get angry. Our team does not win. A movie disappoints us. There is a time for anger—Psalm 4 says to be angry and not sin. Elihu presents himself as angry about their lack of insight, and that seems to be a justifiable thing to be angry about, if anything is. They did not provide meaning and they did not defend God. None of the comforters were able to respond to Job's argument, but Job was also wrong. So Elihu will not use their type of argument, and he says that here. So any view of Elihu that says he is repeating the other three is incorrect. They've been silenced by Job; now he directs himself to Job. It is interesting: Elihu's speech ends in chapter 32 with saying he is not going to engage in flattery, which is empty speech. God judges the flatterers. And the way I think of flattery is in terms of compliments— "Hey, have you've been working out?"—just that kind of thing, as opposed to empty words. Rather, Elihu views flattery as empty words. He isn't going to engage in empty words. I am not going to engage in empty words. I am going to use arguments.

Mediator

Every word of the mouth will be judged by God. This is what Elihu is saying at the end of chapter 32. In chapter 33, directed to Job, Elihu is the mediator, and Job had asked for a mediator. Elihu is going to come in, and we'll see if Job is satisfied with this. Elihu brings his case against Job for what has now come out of the mouth of Job. Job has compounded the original problem. It is not just the beginning issue, way back in chapters 1-3. Now it is Job's responses to his friends and his not having been able to find the meaning that is there in his life.

Elihu tells Job to pay attention to everything he says. The emphasis is not self-centered, as some people might say: "Pay attention to what *I* say." Rather, it is, "Pay attention, Job, to what's going to be said." He is going to affirm in chapter 33 that God does speak. God is not silent. God does call us back from our sins. Pay attention. Elihu affirms our common human condition as part of saying that what he knows, anybody can and should know. So, as a mediator, he is affirming he is like Job. They are both humans. But that also puts responsibility on Job to say, look, what I am saying right now are things you could also know. You should be able to answer me because we are both rational.

What Job Said

Does Elihu get it right? Does he see more clearly than Job here? Look at 33:8. He is going to summarize Job's view. "But you have said in my hearing" (it is kind of evidentiary), "I heard the very words." Let's put those together: "But you said in my hearing, I heard the very words, 'I am pure and without sin. I am clean and free from guilt. Yet God has found fault with me. He considers me his enemy. He fastens my feet in shackles. He keeps close watch on my paths.' But I tell you, Job, in this you are not right." So, did Job say that? I think he did, and Elihu is drawing out the implications of what Job had said in saying that the wicked seem to do well and the righteous suffer. And the whole time along the way, Job is not looking at what sin he might have, but instead saying, I don't deserve this.

In 33:14: "God does speak, now one way, now another." And here's the key in 14b: "Though men may not perceive it." God does speak. And the atheist says, "Not enough evidence, God. I don't see anything." And Sherlock Holmes would say to Dr. Watson, "You see everything; you are just not drawing inferences from what you see." We must have a Sherlockian approach: we start with what is basic and clear. God does speak. And so the burden is not on God for having failed to provide evidences. I saw a Christian humor article with the caption: "Atheist demands evidence for God's existence besides the entire universe." It may be there and we are not seeing it, and that is the key here. 33:14b: You did not see it; you did not see what was there. How many have dulled themselves and don't see that; they are not diligently seeking God?

Insight

We may not perceive what is indeed clear, but that does not mean God is not speaking. And Elihu gives an example next, starting in 33:15. "In a dream, in a vision of the night, when deep sleep falls on men as they slumber in their beds, he may speak in their ears and terrify them with warnings to turn man from wrongdoing and keep him from pride, to preserve his soul from the pit." In an initial reading of that we might be a little bit confused. What is this? Sort of an individual special revelation that some people get dreams? I haven't had any dreams. I want a dream. Well, remember that Eliphaz had brought that up. That was a formative piece for his character, that he had had this religious experience—a spirit had come to him at night. And what that spirit said was incorrect. Eliphaz did not test the spirits. He might make the excuse that he did not have the New Testament—he did not know he was supposed to test the spirits yet. No, that is a general revelation principle: interpret your experiences. So it is not simply any experience, because Eliphaz had that special experience. Here's what I think this is: I do not think it is merely some kind of a dream in special revelation. I think it is about the time in which we are most reflective.

Sometimes we are almost asleep, not quite asleep, or coming out of sleep, and the busyness of the day has passed, that is the time when our mind starts to think about things and wander. Sometimes it is called the "witching hour" because of that. There is a purpose for this time at night. That is the time in which we should be self-reflective about the right kinds of things. These "dreams," what dreams may come on your beds. David speaks about this: prayer on his bed in Psalm 4. What are we doing there, and what way does God speak there? We should be able to reflect on our life there. I do not think it only means to lay there waiting for a vision of some kind. Are we able to reflect on our life? There is a purpose for it, in verses 17 and 18: "To turn you from wrongdoing and keep you from pride." Matthew Henry uses this term for it: conscience. The pangs of conscience. And that, again, might be a word that we narrow to certain things. Elihu was using it in a broad sense that I am using it, which is, this reflection time that comes when we are no longer busy during the day. God speaks to us there to keep us from pride. But, in verse 14b, "you did not perceive it." I did not hear an audible voice. No, it is not an audible voice. It is to preserve you from pride and your soul from the pit.

So, God does speak. That is one example Elihu gives. What did you learn during those times of reflection? Anything at all? No, not at all; I just took some more melatonin and went back to bed. Sometimes that is the nicest time of the day; if one can get up earlier, a few hours before everybody else, and have that time to read and reflect. What did we learn? That is one way Elihu gives, one example, what would we know if we reflected.

Then secondly, that man may be chastened on a bed of pain. So the first one was a bed of reflection; now we are to the bed of pain. Either way, those are the two options. Either way, this is great—no matter what we are doing, God is speaking to us. We can't avoid it. "With constant distress in his bones, so that his very being finds food repulsive, and his soul loathes the choicest meal. His flesh wastes away to nothing and his bones, once hidden, now stick out." This is the suffering Job is in. God is speaking through suffering. How can that be?

Verse 22: "His soul draws near to the pit and his life to the messengers of death." Again, I think verses 17 and 18 still apply: suffering is to turn us from pride (the opposite of pride is the fear of the Lord) and preserve our soul from the pit. Whereas here in 22, his soul is drawing near to the pit. And then in 23—I think this is the third one, but it is building on that second one: "If there is an angel on his side, a messenger, as a mediator, one out of a thousand, to tell a man what is right for him, to be gracious to him and say, spare him from going down to the pit; I have found a ransom for him." Keep that in mind: this requires a ransom, a payment. "Then his flesh is renewed like a child's." Renewed flesh, renewed heart. "It is restored, as in the days of his youth.

He prays to God and finds favor with him. He sees God's face and shouts for joy. He is restored by God to his righteous state. Then he comes to men and says, I sinned, and I perverted what is right. But I did not get what I deserved; he redeemed my soul from going down to the pit, and I will live to enjoy the light" (v28).

Repentance, ransom, and atonement, end up in this person being able to say, I was spared from the pit. And this confession of sin—I sinned, I perverted what is right. And look at what Elihu says Job's sin is, compared to the three comforters. He is not accusing Job of gross fruit sins, gross violations of the law. He comes back to overcoming that pride, which is the opposite of the fear of the Lord: I sinned in that way, and I perverted what is right. But I did not get what I deserved.

God speaks here. He speaks on our ability to reflect, he speaks in suffering—the bed of reflection, the bed of suffering—and in redemption itself. "God does all these things to a man twice, even three times, to turn back his soul from the pit so that the light of life may shine on him" (30). What is that light of life? He said it also in verse 28: enjoy the light. That which makes God known.

See God's Face

In 33:26, he says "to see God's face." What does it mean to end up seeing God's face? He refers to a light in verse 28, and then in verse 30: to turn back his soul to the light of life. The exact phrase is used in John 1:4, that knowledge of God, to know God. That is what Job must learn to repent of. He rightly defended himself against the three comforters and what they accused him of. But what will he say to this from Elihu? Has Job sought God as he should have? If he had done so then he would be able to show the glory of God from the works of God. Elihu speaks here of sin but also repentance from that sin and restoration to the knowledge of God.

And Elihu says, pay attention Job, listen to me. Be silent and I will speak. If you have anything to say, answer me. We might wonder what's going on. He says, be silent; answer me. Focus on the argument Job, and respond to it. Speak up for yourself. For I want you to be cleared. But if not, then listen; be silent, and I will teach you wisdom. This is profound. This chapter, 33, shows how Elihu deals with this knowledge of God that is present and the responsibility to know God and to find life in that light. Elihu gives an example of sin and repentance. Later, we'll look carefully at what Job does and see if Job follows Elihu's advice. That is one way to know if Elihu is a good guy or bad guy.

You Men of Learning

In chapter 34, Elihu now turns to the friends, the comforters. Elihu had initially brought action against Job. The book is structured in a kind of legal format. People love Law and Order, don't they? What if they had the Job version? Action is being brought. Job, Elihu says, you did not speak what is right. Now to these wise men he says: "Hear my words; listen to me, you men of learning. For the ear tests words as the tongue tastes food. Let us discern for ourselves what is right and learn together what is good" (34:2-4) This really is the focus of the book. What is good? Given the role Job should have in philosophy, this should replace Book 7 of the Republic and the Allegory of the Cave. That is about Plato's view of the good; this is about the good and how we know it. Plato speaks of a direct vision of the good apart from the world or the body. That is not the knowledge of God from the works of God. How do we get to this? In verse 5, Job says, "'I am innocent, but God denies me justice. Although I am right, I am considered a liar. Although I am guiltless, his arrow inflicts an incurable wound.' What man is like Job, who drinks scorn like water?" Elihu asks.

Is this too heavy? Job keeps company with evildoers. He associates with wicked men, for he says, it profits a man nothing when he tries to please God. Is that right? These verses are why some commentators lump Elihu as a fourth accuser just like the other three. He is bringing accusation here, but I think he is correctly identifying Job's position. Job said, the wicked often seem to get away with it and the righteous suffer. What's the implication of that? "Then what's the point?" Asaph had a similar problem in Psalm 73, and many people wonder what the point is. If I can get the same outcome by not being good, which takes effort, why not do it? Why be good? No one notices. I mean, I try to do all my good deeds so people see them, but no one pays attention. It is frustrating. So, what is the purpose? It profits man nothing. So now we are going to get into an argument about that in 34:10. What we are seeing is, as I said, the father of philosophy addressing the beginning of philosophy, which is the fear of the Lord. And we are seeing it applied in the life of a person.

Elihu is drawing out this implication of what Job said. He calls Job wicked for claiming that God does not have consequences for the wicked--that is why Job is "associating with wicked men." The wicked say that same thing—God does not hear. Asaph goes over this in Psalm 73. I call them the biblical atheists. There is no God, they say. He does nothing. He does not see. And Job was also saying the wicked do not suffer. This is wrong. "Listen to me, you men of understanding: far be it from God to do evil" (34:10).

Let's take a look at Elihu's method. He begins with basic things. Here is one: far be it from God to do evil. That is a given from general revelation. We know that going into scripture, so if something appears as if God is doing evil, it is only appearance, and it is a mistake. Far be it from God, who is perfect in power and goodness, to do evil. That is indubitable. The beginning point. Far be it from the Almighty to do wrong. "He repays a man for what he has done; he brings upon him what his conduct deserves. It is unthinkable that God would do wrong, that the Almighty would pervert justice. Who appointed him over the earth? Who put him in charge of the whole world? If it were his intention, and he withdrew his Spirit and breath, all mankind would perish together, and man return to the dust" (11-15).

God is not an elected official. God is not supported by humans or given his role by humans. God is the creator of all things ex nihilo. He gave them being. And he looked and they were very good. There is no one else to trust besides God, and that trust is never misplaced. But, as we saw in chapter 32, we may not perceive what's going on, and because we do not do that, we may draw false conclusions about God, which is the problem Job is now in.

But as we go through these same sufferings, we bring this back to our mind: God is perfectly just. That is a given. So now Elihu will give an argument, starting in 34:16. This is interesting, because I think this is kind of a moral governance argument from the five ways (of Aquinas), so to speak. "If you have understanding, hear this; listen to what I say. Can he who hates justice govern? Will you condemn the Just and Mighty One? Is he not the one who says to kings, you are worthless, and nobles, you are wicked? Who shows no partiality to princes and does not favor the rich over the poor? For they are all the work of his hands. They die in an instant, in the middle of the night. The people are shaken and they pass away. The mighty are removed without human hand."

If we are in the realm of saying God is the creator and the ruler, then from there we do not have any ability to say somehow God is unjust. God is ruling justly. And the reason why we may not have perceived it is because we did not keep the correct end in mind. Again, a little version of this is Psalm 73. Asaph says the same things about the wicked and goes through some similar kinds of wrestlings. The wicked seem to prosper. They seem to do well. And when we went over that section, I agreed with that. I defended Job and said, yes, they do seem to do well. Is that infuriating? Well, on one level, in the worldly sense. But remember the pit—that their life is going down to the pit. And in that sense, they are suddenly washed away. Even the earthly fame they may attain could be taken away instantly, quickly.

But wanting this person to lose their wealth and lose their prestige should not be our focus. Where are they at in respect to that light of life? *That* is the good. And on that, they are absent. And that is what Asaph came to see as he reflected on the temple—the revelation in the temple about the vicarious work of God in atonement.

God Rules

God rules. He rules over princes. Princes are only in place to serve the purpose of God for a time. But like everything else, they too are judged by God. It is a mighty judgment, and it should not be missed. We may have missed it and not seen it. It'd be interesting to look back at the newspapers; just pick a year—1810. What was animating the people for those months? And then ask, without letting someone read it, to name some things that people were worried about in 1810. Political machinations going on, that are now washed away. Gone to history's memory. Someone might say, "I don't care about those, but I care about the current ones—those are what really matter. The wicked today are not getting just punishment." Well, can't we imagine it will be the same in a few decades? What was so important just washed away. What matters, what is permanent, is the rule of God. Are we perceiving that? Look at this in 34:21: "His eye is on the ways of men; he sees their every step."

This is another fixed point. God is omniscient. Do we think God does not know? That is what the biblical atheist says. He says God does not know and God does not care. Are we taking company with that guy?

No. God is omniscient. He sees their every step. For the Lord God omnipotent reigneth. There is no dark place, no deep shadow, where evildoers can hide. God has no need to examine men further that they should come before him for judgment. This is biblical atheism. We might say somehow there is a God, but then in the same breath, say he does not rule, he does not know what's going on, he is not paying attention—look at this guy over here—he is getting away with something. Where is God? No. Elihu brings us back to remind us of basic things. God knows all things. He sees what all people do. Every word will be judged. The kind of judgment we want may not be the one that is happening. God is bringing us back through our self-deception, through self-justification, to root sin, before him. That is the judgment. But can't he also topple the powerful? He has and does. But in this chapter, we are looking at this kind of sin.

"He punishes them for their wickedness wherever anyone can see them." And then in 34:29: "If he remains silent, who can condemn him? If he hides his face, who can see him?" That is a kind of judgment, when God hides his face. "He is over man and nation alike, to keep a godless man from ruling, from laying snares for the people. Suppose a man says to God, I am guilty, but will offend no more. Teach me what I cannot see. If I have done wrong, I will not do so again. Should God then reward you on your terms?" Elihu is comparing now. This is the second time he is given an example of repentance. Suppose a man repents and asks God for help and forgiveness. And then it is on God to tell him how atonement will happen. But you want God to do things on your terms, Job. Is that how things should work, when you refuse to repent? 34:33b: "You must decide, not I. So tell me what you know. Men of understanding declare, wise men hear what I say. Job speaks without knowledge. His words lack insight."

Job's Condition?

I don't like reading that about Job, but Elihu is right. "Oh, that Job might be tested to the utmost for answering like a wicked man." Tested to the utmost. Is that what he is going through? I think it is to the utmost. "For answering like a wicked man." What was in Job's heart was brought out, in his words. "To his sin (what was originally there), he is added rebellion. Scornfully he claps his hands among us and multiplies his words against God" (34:37). Rebellion. So, is Elihu just piling on with the three comforters? Or is he getting to something new here that they did not get to at all? A deeper call for repentance? I think the answer to that is here, but the answer is going to be what Job does as well. Job gives his answer to Elihu. It is a very different answer than he gave to the three friends.

Elihu now takes apart Job's claims. Do you think this is just, Job? You say, I'll be cleared by God. Job wants a trial where God comes down and there is a court case and Job is cleared. "You ask him, 'What profit is it to me, and what do I gain by not sinning?'" That shows a very fundamental misunderstanding. What profit is there in not sinning? Elihu asks. I'd like to reply to you and to your friends with you. "Look up at the heavens and see; gaze at the clouds so high above you. If you sin, how does it affect God?" And he goes through a list of things like that. What does that mean, "What profit is it to me?" Job's idea is that God has laid down these rules, and when he sins it somehow affects God—God loses something.

I remember there was a Star Trek episode where they encountered the old Greek gods who had somehow derived power from human prayer. When humans stopped praying to them, they lost their power and went away to an alien world. Is that what it is—God gets power from us keeping his rules or something? What profit is there for God? Job, if you sin, how does it affect him? If your sins are many, what does that do to him? Or what if you are righteous? What do you give to God? Or what does he receive from your hand? Your wickedness only affects a man like yourself, and your righteousness only the sons of men.

There are inherent consequences in sin, connected back to chapter 33, and the pit. The failure to see that light, to have life. How could we ask what the consequences of sin are? Or what does it profit to be righteous? We have not understood righteousness then, have we? Righteousness is life. It is the path of life.

Two Paths

There are these two paths only. God is not the one profiting from righteousness. This is our only path to life. 35:9: all the people crying out and saying, where is God in the history of the world? "Men cry out under a load of oppression. They plead for relief from the arm of the powerful. But no one says, 'Where is God my maker, who gives songs in the night (notice that night—remember the dreams earlier, when we should be reflecting and thinking), who teaches more to us than to the beasts of the earth, and makes us wiser than the birds of the air?'" No one says that, do they? They cry out under oppression. It is not fair, this other person owns all the capital; I have been alienated from the output of my labor. I have been alienated from the means of production. It is not fair, it is not right. They cry out for those sorts of things, right? We need to form a group so that Pharaoh can't keep making us build pyramids without equal pay, better pay.

They Do Not Seek God

People do not say, where is God, who is my teacher, whom I should repent to and love? I don't hear that when I read through the history. No one seeks God (35:10). They want relief from their suffering. They want the kingdom, but they don't want God in it. And that is the response to what Job said earlier: "He is not answering my prayers." I pressed that point, saying, isn't that right? God does not seem to answer prayers. Where is God? Well, people aren't praying like this, are they? That is a prayer Asaph gave also (in psalm 73). And that is the prayer of David. It does not always mean a certain kind of suffering ends, but it means we come to know God. We have that life, which is the light.

He does not answer when men cry because of the arrogance of the wicked. That is an arrogant thing to say: "God, release me from suffering, but I don't want to let go of my sin." That is wicked. God does not listen to their empty pleas. The Almighty pays no attention. And here's a key verse directed to Job: 35:14: "How much less then will he listen when you say that you do not see him?" Where is God? I do not see him. Not enough evidence, God. Imagine the wickedness of saying, if I were ever confronted by God and asked why I don't believe, I would say, "There is not enough evidence, God. I don't perceive you. I don't see you." Well, Elihu says, I would not expect someone like you, Job, to see God. Someone lost in their sins who's not seeking. It would shock me if someone who does not seek God saw God. So, of course, you don't. And that is the condition: no one seeks God. We don't see him, so we must wait for him.

The Condemnation

In 35:16 Elihu says "Job opens his mouth with empty talk. Without knowledge, he multiplies words." This is the condemnation of Elihu. This is a different kind of condemnation than the other three friends. Here is root sin. Empty words, vanity. You justified yourself, Job, and you did not justify God. You should have known that God was your patient and loving teacher. In fact, in Amos chapter 4 we can see that God is talking to Israel about how he is wooed them. The chapter is filled with natural evil. I took away your rain, God says, and you did not turn to me. I left you to yourself and you did not turn to me. All of these instances of natural evil on the people of Israel and they did not turn to him. God's instructing them; God's calling them back to him. That is the root sin, and that is what Job does have to repent of. Amos 4. Then in chapter 36, there is more to say about God. Chapters 36 and 37 are going to transition us right into chapter 38, and that is going to be moving. I can't even tell you what happens in 38 yet. There is more to say about God. Elihu says this: "Bear with me a little longer and I'll show you that there is more to be said on God's behalf. I get my knowledge from afar; I will ascribe justice to my maker. Be assured that my words are not false. One perfect in knowledge is with you" (36:1-4)

How do we take that? I think the sense of "perfect" knowledge is clear or certain. Given Elihu's method and how he is proceeding, he does have that. It is not a boast about "I am perfect, look at what I've attained" as opposed to "look what's there; you could have done this and should have done this." You should know these things, Job. How old are you? The Fool said to King Lear: You should not have grown old until you grew wise.

In 36:5, Elihu goes back to the bedrock, the elementary things, the basics—God is mighty, but does not despise men. He is mighty and firm in his purpose. What is his purpose? Well, his purpose was to let me lead a nice life. Remember back when Job was talking about the nice life he wanted, the life of prosperity? Health and wealth, eventually to be gathered up in his bed with his kids around him. And there is nothing wrong with that kind of desire. It is almost weird if someone does not want that. But to put it in that place of prominence—that is not God's purpose for you. God's purpose for you is that you might know him and overcome root sin. Here Elihu goes through a list of how God does that. We can relate this back to what Eliphaz said. Eliphaz's argument was, God is so high above us that all men are just wicked by being what they are. And that is not the position Elihu takes. God is above us, God is almighty, but he does not despise us. He works in each of our lives in a personal manner to call us to him. And if you perceived what God had been doing, Job, you would see how it had been tailor-made, how he had been working to call you back. If we do not listen, we die in that condition.

The Darkened Mind

In 36:14, Elihu says, "They die in their youth." The NIV says it this way. Usually the King James is the one that just tells it straight, but the NIV was a little more straight this time. "They die in their youth among male prostitutes of the shrine." That is about as bad as it gets for the wicked. A description of utter vanity and wickedness—that is the end of the wicked who do not pay attention to God. But those who suffer he delivers from their suffering; he speaks to them in their affliction. And he uses this word "wooing" in verse 16, which is why I connected it to Amos 4, which uses a similar idea: "He is wooing you from the jaws of distress to a spacious place free from restriction. But now you are laden with judgment due to the wicked. Judgment and justice have taken hold of you" (v16-17). Because of these views of God, Job has to repent. God is perfectly just and he doubted that. That should be our starting point. And those who go in that path and doubt God and they say there is no God, or God does not see what we do, God does not act—they end here. That is where they end in Romans 1 also. Utter wickedness and a dead-end road. Wickedness goes nowhere. Male prostitutes at the shrine. What are they doing with themselves? Worshiping idols and destroying their bodies. That is the end of the road. That is where wickedness culminates. Unbelief is without excuse, and it does not stay at the level of unbelief—it will manifest itself in our life.

God As Teacher

But we have seen twice already from Elihu the example of what it would be like to repent before God. He says in 21, "Beware of turning to evil, which you seem to prefer to affliction." Isn't that interesting—people prefer evil to the suffering that takes them out of the evil. That was the prayer of those under oppression: just get me out of the oppression. But none seek God. Then in 22: "God is exalted in his power. Who is a teacher like him?" This is the second time God is our teacher. And the best commentaries I read bring that out about Elihu (saying God is our teacher) but they do not yet get to that distinction between root and fruit sin. It is not just teaching about sin or just about fruit sin; God is a teacher getting us back to root sin. That is a teacher who hasn't burned out after five or six years. God is still your teacher. He hasn't burned out yet. He hasn't just assigned you to the dumb-dumb pile and put you in the corner with a dunce hat. He is continuing to work in your life to bring you to reflect on that root sin. God is a teacher.

And who is a teacher like him? If we ever want to look to a master teacher, who else would we look to? But many people may not see it. They say, I do not see God teaching anybody. Look at the wicked; they are running rampant. It is even worse now—this is the worst generation ever. Well, you are not seeing it. Job is not seeing it. God addressed that earlier—or Elihu did. It is clear what God is doing and you do not see it, Job, which is a double problem for you: you are both doing it and you do not see it. That is a problem.

The work of God in teaching that we should so we should extol the work of God and find our meaning in knowing this. This is a command—36:24: "Remember to extol the work of God, which men have praised in song." And since Job's time we get a whole book of them! Isn't that nice? Psalms extolling the work of God.

All mankind has seen it. Men gaze on it from afar. How great is God—beyond our understanding. There are things incomprehensible. The number of his years has passed finding out. He is eternal. This is general revelation Elihu is appealing to here—not just because he does not have a Bible, but because these things are things all men can know about God. You should be extolling the works of God, Job. That is how Job should have ended rather than the way he did end in an accusation.

The Purpose of Suffering

From 36:27 continuing on through chapter 37, Elihu is preparing the same kind of thing that God is going to say. 36:27: "He draws up the drops of water, which distill as rain in the streams." The particulars of creation reveal God the Creator. Suffering serves a purpose. The purpose of suffering is a callback. The word here used is "wooing." It gives the sense of one who loves us, wooing us. The purpose of suffering is that: to teach us. And it refers to Job as well.

Then Elihu will get into, "Have you considered the works of God?" Remember the beginning, "Have you considered my servant Job?" Now we get into the section of this book which is about this: have you considered the works of God? This is different than when the others brought up the works of God earlier in the book. They brought it up just to emphasize the sovereignty of God. And that is what we'll be wrestling with in the next chapter. Does not God just show up and show he is powerful and Job has to say, yes, sir? No. Job and his friends already know the sovereignty of God. They already know the omnipotence of God. And when they spoke about it earlier, it was more like that. God's powerful; who are you to question him? Here we are going to ask, have we seen the glory of God displayed in the creation—the intricacies of the creation, the wisdom of the creation? Have we seen that? Have we paid attention to it? Some see it and they get stuck there and, therefore, miss a lot of it.

God Is Known in Creation: Consider the Works of God

Some ignore creation and they look to go to the superlunary areas. The celestial spheres. We should be extolling the works of God here and now. Elihu gives some examples here. This is not just God's power or hiddenness; this is the details of God. It evokes awe, which is the word for the fear of God. The awe of God, in the face of the Sublime. And it is sublime. These chapters are. The creation is. The providence of God is. But it is also cognitive—because some people (the mystics) stop at the non-cognitive as if it is just an experience. It is cognitive; we do know God and we should know God. And that is the sin that Job is being called back from. Elihu says in 37:1, "At this my heart pounds and leaps from his place." This is what he is excited about: thinking about the wisdom of God in creation.

What gets us excited? Not much anymore. No, listen! Listen to the roar of his voice and the rumbling that comes from his mouth as he sends it to the ends of the earth, as you see this wisdom of God. "When his voice resounds, he holds back nothing. God's voice thunders in marvelous ways. He does great things beyond our understanding. He says of the snow, 'Fall on the earth,' and to the rain shower, 'Be a mighty downpour'" (v4-6). Have we thought about these? The animals that take cover? They remain in their den. The power of lightning? Have we somehow moved past that because we have come to understand electrons? No, there is no God the creator and designer; there are electrons. Or someone says "God" and we say "but electrons." And somehow, we have moved beyond that with science—we have overcome this ignorance. We think we know all about the material cause. If anything, it just adds another thing where we say, wow, God made those.

And it is an interesting comparison to Baal, which will come later—he is supposed to be the god of lightning. So anytime in the Psalms or Job where there is mention of thunder and lightning like this, higher critics will say, see, this is the Hebrews stealing from the Canaanites. No, it is actually the other way around. We know from general revelation there isn't a fellow like Baal.

Chapter 37:14: "Listen to this, Job. Stop and consider God's wonders." Just that. Listen to this, Job. Stop and consider God's wonders. Have you considered God's servant Job? Have you considered the wonders of God? No? Well, God is wooing us back from root sin to consider those things. "Tell us what we should say to him" (v 19a).

Now we are getting to the conclusion. Instantly, in verse 15, Elihu begins something. Keep this in mind. "Do you know how God controls the clouds and makes his lightning flash?" And then the next one. Questions. Elihu is preparing the way. Guess what God is going to do? Before this, Job was making declarations about creation. Sometimes I can see my students sitting there like they are paying attention and they are not; they are pretending to pay attention. They have the "I am paying attention" face on. But then when I question them, it is going to change the dynamic. Why does God use questions? Here Elihu sets up the context for when God will question. He starts using questions. Have you considered this, Job? That makes a person respond; they can't just nod. Have you considered these things?

Chapter 37:19 gets us closer to a conclusion. "Tell us what we should say to him. We cannot draw up our case because of our darkness. Should it be told that I want to speak? Would any man ask to be swallowed up?" We could be swallowed up by God in this presumption. And guess what's going to happen in the next chapters? "No one can look at the sun, bright as it is in the skies after the wind has swept them clean out of the north. He comes in golden splendor. God comes in almighty majesty" (v21-22) Think about that; I mentioned Plato's allegory of the cave—his use of the sun vs. this use, which is just like Psalm 19. The sun reminds us of God. And who could look at the sun? Who could look at God? The sun is the greatest creation of God in the sense of the most powerful one in our experience. Can we look at the sun, as bright as it is? You should have known God, Plato. That is why this is superior in the sense that this gets into what we can and should have known about God. Now, the conclusion: "The Almighty is beyond our reach and exalted in power. In his justice and great righteousness he does not oppress" (v23). That is the issue, and Elihu is refuting Job on that point. He does not oppress you, Job. He has been teaching you. He has been wooing you. "Therefore, men revere him." That is the basis for our fear of God, our love of God. Does he not have regard for all those who are wise in heart? And yet Job has made these accusations.

Job Is Silent

We do not hear from Job now, which is notable since he responded to the others. Elihu has prepared the way, but Job does not get a reply in at this point. Job showed that the solutions of his friends were worthless. He is asked us for meaning, which is good—he was right in doing that. But then he argued that in this life, the wicked prosper. He did not see the rule of God, and he did not justify God. Job asked for a mediator and Elihu mediated. Is that what he expected? But Elihu also affirmed that he is just a man like Job. He is not some kind of supernatural being, and he pointed to the need for God to make things right.

Elihu is a man; he knows these things; we could have known them. God must provide a ransom. We must repent from sin, from not seeing God, and then from justifying ourselves over God. How many times have we done that? And there must be a ransom for our sin. Elihu told Job what Job should have told his friends. And now there is no pause between Elihu ending and

God entering the story. In the next part: "Then the Lord answered Job out of the storm." Are you ready? Hear the words of Elihu to prepare the way.

Job Part Six

God Speaks

40:6-8

Then the Lord spoke to Job out of the storm: "Brace yourself like a man; I will question you, and you shall answer me. Would you discredit my justice? Would you condemn me to justify yourself?"

Why does God respond to Job's question with questions? Job asked to confront God and now here is the rise in the action. We have gone through the dialogue with the comforters and we spent time on the wrangling back and forth, because we needed to get into those details and make that come to life for us as we read through Job. And we saw Elihu's response. Job had asked for a mediator and he got one—and was silenced. Job responded to his comforters in some detail. After Elihu, that was it. There was no response. Now there is a transition from Elihu to God.

The dispute we are looking at involves disagreements between four otherwise pious men. So although we won't be looking much at those first three now, we'll be returning to them as we think about the outcome of Job's comforters. What would it take to have unity between them? And we are told what it would take in chapter 42. What is the resolution of the dispute? We have a lot to unpack here because God speaks. What will God say and why will he say it this way?

This is a profound section of scripture. That could be said of any section of scripture in one sense, but think about what occurs here. Has this ever happened in the history of the world that God would speak to someone like this? We can think of other similar cases, maybe Abraham or Moses, and this is not to somehow set those as lesser, but to think about what happens here, at such an early part of human history. Here we have Job, who is *not* in that line of Abraham, as the most righteous. Righteous Job, patient Job. And it is precisely because he is those things that he is able to endure this. Others would not have made it.

We might reflect on ourselves: when we go through suffering, are we quick to complain and talk about how hard it is and maybe it is not fair? If we are able to be objective about the threshold we are at when we said that, and think of where Job was at, we'll see how we couldn't have gone through what he did. I couldn't have endured what Job did. But Job did, precisely because of his righteousness, blamelessness, and integrity. That is the interesting twist on it. His friends will say, because you are the greatest of sinners, look what you are going through. Ah, but perhaps because of who he is he is able to go through this and is pushed further. The revelation is pushed further for all of us because of what Job goes through.

And here we have just this beginning of God's questions. It is almost hard to speak. "Then the Lord answered Job out of the storm." Then Yahweh speaks to Job. We have the covenantal name of God used, the redemptive name of God. Think about that. That second person of the Trinity the Word of God who makes God known. The words of God are going to make God known here. We are going to look at them just like we did the other ones. But I want to first ask, how do we understand these sections?

Five Common Views of What God Is Doing

I would hope at this time that the reader has gone through Job before in their life. I am relying on some background knowledge and familiarity with how people have spoken about its solution. And I wonder if people have found commentators' solutions adequate. I am not asking if Job's solution is adequate—I mean how do people understand Job? Are they getting Job when they talk about it? I have come across a few examples of what commentators say God is doing.

The first says God is showing his power to silence Job. God flexes, and people take these questions that way. Who are you, Job? You should just be quiet because of this power, in the face of the power of God. The questions are to humble Job. And we have to look at that, because there is a humbling that goes on. But is it because of the power of God? And why might someone reduce the answer to power? I have heard professors say this, people who view themselves as having studied quite a bit, say that this is what Job is about. Job is about God silencing questions. Do not ask questions. Or, since some of these are related, but they are a little different: overwhelming Job, but not answering him. It is around 70-plus questions, and it could just be this flood against Job. You have a question for me about why I do things, Job? I'll open the floodgates and flood you with questions.

A second view considers God as a skeptic. He is kind of skirting the issue, sidetracking it, not being direct. One might wonder, why does not God just be direct here? Job asked a question; just tell us an answer in three or four sentences. I am going to address that, because that is a good question about why God does this the way he does. And maybe we have suggestions for God. But I am taking it as a given: however, God did it, that is the right way to do it—so let's figure out why. Why does God approach it this way?

Number three is that the questions are simply to establish God's authority. This comes often from people who put this book into the polytheism of its neighbors. God, like Zeus, is somewhat worried about rivals and has to establish that he is the chief god. He is in charge. This is especially true for those who see Behemoth and Leviathan as spiritual powers—maybe even Canaanite gods. The context of Job will tell us that these are a continuation of references to creatures in nature rather than a sudden shift from the creation to spirits (Satan) or spiritual states (death). Nor can this be an attempt to situate God in the Canaanite worldview, which sets aside all we know from clear general revelation and the Biblical Worldview in Genesis 1-3. The idea that these are spiritual beings or spiritual states is another part of the view that this is an attempt by God to show his power. In these solutions I am going over the standard of literalism on one hand and allegoricalism on the other.

Fourth: God's purpose of why he asks questions and does not give answers is to undermine Job's legal ability to bring a case. You have no legal standing, Job—and legal terminology has been used in this case. We'll hear about that sometimes in federal cases; someone will say a person does not have standing to bring their case. That is not a comment on the case; perhaps if someone with standing brought it then it would go through and they'd be proven right. But this is not the person who's able to do that. So that is another view of what God's purpose to do here is, in that he enters into the legal courtroom and undermines Job's standing as a defendant.

And then fifth, that these questions are a kind of antiquated "God of the gaps" answer. Even if it were a good answer back then, for illiterate peasants, it does not help us now because we know the answers to most of these questions God asks. We figured them out. We know about where light comes from, etc. Is science able to fill in these questions? Is that a weakness in God's argument that science could fill in? Do we know how this happens? Well, actually, yes. Photons bounce off things etc. This is a God of the gaps type argument.

Notice how none of these wrestles with what is clear about God from general revelation. We come to the text already knowing that only God is eternal, knowing about the infinite power, knowledge, and goodness of God, knowing that original creation was very good, knowing that moral evil is permitting to deepen the revelation of God's justice and mercy, knowing that natural evil is a call back from moral evil. Job too had access to clear general revelation and all of these truths. He knew in the early parts of the book that God is sovereign over all things. Any reading of Job that says God is teaching him about sovereignty isn't addressing what was already there. If a reader comes to Job as a fideist then a fideist reading will be the outcome. If a reader comes to Job as a skeptic then a skeptical reading will be the outcome. If a reader comes to Job knowing that there is a clear general revelation of God's eternal power and divine nature then there is a much deeper message to see here that applies to all humans as they wrestle with the problem of evil and come to the teachings of scripture.

God's Answer to Those in Self-Deception and Self-Justification

God answers Job's question with a series of questions. Why is God answering in this way? Why isn't God being direct? What is the theme throughout all of this? What is being highlighted is the reality of sin, self-deception and self-justification, and the need for natural evil to get through all of those. We looked at those last two: self-deception and self-justification. That is what Job's comforters did not get to. They got to sins, specifically. But when authority is there and exercised, we deceive ourselves about it, we blame, and we say "I am in the right and God's wrong," and we justify ourselves. "Look how God's acting. God has been heavy-handed to me. God has been cruel to me. He is lost his temper with me. I did not deserve this." And that now has compounded the original problem: that we are not seeking. Now we have got more problems on our hands that we have to deal with. We have deceived ourselves; we have justified ourselves at the expense of God, and God's going to ask Job about that specifically, that he did that. You justified yourself at my expense, Job.

When we looked at Elihu, we felt the pain of what Job is going through, and especially the rebuke of Elihu—he was right and Job was wrong. However, we are changing course now. The perspective is different, because empathy can be misleading. Empathy focuses on how feelings operate, and feelings can operate out of self-deception and self-justification. Now we hear God speaking, and we'd better pay attention to what God says and what Job has done, and why all these events in Job's life are justified. Because there is that legal terminology of what God is doing here and why it is for Job's good. And Job did not simply miss that; he compounded it with problems, with things about God that we are going to look at—what Job said about God. And so, the perspective now is not simply our brother Job, who is righteous (though that is there), but now it is: how has Job responded to the discipline of God? And what does God have to say? This theme in the book again, the thesis: What does it take to get our focus, to get our attention? What does it take? And we may have thought it takes a lot less, but this is the most righteous man and this is what it took to get him to focus.

God speaks from the storm, from the whirlwind. "Who is this that darkens my counsel with words without knowledge? Brace yourself like a man. I will question you and you shall answer me" (38:2). Be a man. Have we ever been told that? "Be a man." Have we ever been called effeminate as a man? "You are not being a man; be one." It is interesting to see what God thinks is a man. A man is someone who understands things and who can answer. I don't think this is literally narrowed down to a masculine man. It is a human. Be a human. But I have heard that challenge before: be a man. And it has to do with being physically tough...well, then you'll lose in comparison to the lion who's going to come up. He is tougher than you. No, to be a man is to be able to answer. And God is going to ask Job, do you understand? You would have understanding if you were a man. Prepare yourself, Job. Are you ready for this? You asked about defending yourself before God; now you get to. To be a man is to show understanding; it is to give proofs. Here we have an intense test. In Genesis 1-3 we talk about the test from the serpent to Adam and Eve. It was one question, one somewhat simple, true/false question. And we might think, that was so difficult, or maybe there would have been more follow-up questions if Adam would have gotten that one right. But here we have a test. How would we do with this test? How would we stand up? Would we want to have an oral quiz by God to defend ourselves? We must show that we do understand.

Job, Meaning, and the Foundation

Job wanted meaning from the beginning. This trial does not make any sense; it is not fair to me. His friends' solution was, you are a sinner, and this is what happens to sinners. And Job gave counterexamples to show that does not make any sense either; this is still not fair. How can we make sense of it? So now we are going to see how God helps us make sense of it.

Job compounded his claims by accusing God of things. God answers those accusations. Look where God starts—this is fascinating to me. 38:4: "Where were you when I laid the earth's foundations? Tell me if you understand." Do you know what God wants to know? Is the foundation in place? Where were you when that foundation was made? God starts with the foundation of all things. When I read commentators, they said ancient people used to think earth was on these pillars, so it is saying God hoisted up these heavy pillars and put the earth on top of it. That is allegoricalism. This is Job. Job's a theist, not a polytheist. He was accused of worshiping the sun, but he is not a sun worshiper. The "foundations of all things": in the beginning, God created the heavens and the earth. This is not just the physical planet and some things above it. All things. Where were you when the foundation was laid, Job? Do you have the foundation in place—and what is it? Who marked off its dimensions? Who stretched a measuring line across it?

This is the immensity of creation. Think about those first verses of Genesis. God created the heavens and the earth. The Spirit hovered over the waters, and imagine the dimensions of what that would have been like. The creation was very good, without evil. But now there is evil—why? Surely, you know, Job. And how do we take "surely you know"? There is a presumption that Job has displayed in his accusations against God. In his self-deception and self-justification, he is become presumptuous. So, we can ask the person who has put themselves forward. Well, you must know. Tell me. You must understand. You must be in the place of a teacher of God.

But I don't take God's questions entirely to be rhetorical. I think that this is a list of questions all of us can spend our days meditating on. God gives us a study guide and we can reflect back and think on these questions. What is the foundation? I wasn't there when it was made—what did God do? How did God lay the foundation? And I do not want to limit that to gravity and certain elements that work in these ways. It includes that, but it is not limited to that. The foundation of all things. God created all other things, but he is beginning here. God is beginning with the most basic thing that could be said about God: only God is eternal. If God lays the foundation of things, that is the beginning of all else. Only God is eternal. That is where he begins by inference or by implication.

The Nature of God the Creator

God starts with the foundation. Who laid the foundation and what is it? God alone is eternal and God alone can create ex nihilo. This is the beginning of the clarity of general revelation. It is no wonder God starts here. We can infer a lot from the nature of God as creator. This is not merely power; it is also knowledge and goodness. One can ask, "Well, how can we know that?" I think we can show that from the eternality of God. God is perfect, not just in power, but in knowledge and goodness, and those are going to be brought out here. God cannot be eternal and also finite in knowledge, or finite in goodness. God as creator determines the nature of a thing and in doing that God determines what is good for that thing. Job was evidencing biblical atheism: the one who says maybe there is a God, but he is not ruling well. The world is in disarray. If I were in charge, it would not look like this. Where is God? And God is responding to that question about his rule and the wisdom of God. And if we do not get the clarity of general revelation in place as our highest good, we will miss this in Job.

One of the things for how this is put together is, "let him who has ears to hear, hear." Why does Christ speak in parables? When persons who do not begin with the clarity of general revelation then tell me what Job is about, I see how much they miss it. The atheist saying that it is about how God is a tyrant and we must set our own moral compass. Maybe someone could get the message of Job more wrong, but it would be hard. I could put that as a challenge for him— "you couldn't get it more wrong." The atheist will say: "Oh, yes, I could— just watch."

So we start with the foundation of what we can know of God and the eternality of God. God goes through things in this chapter that are comparable to the days of creation, though the order does not follow that exactly. Then God says: "who shut the sea behind doors when it burst forth from the womb? When I made the cloud its garment and wrapped it in thick darkness?" (v8-9). The beginning. This is not just the sea simpliciter. That is how Zeus finds it—there is already the sea, and then he has to somehow subdue it. This is not polytheism of any form; including those who try to find the Canaanite religion here. This is the beginning of the sea when it burst forth from the womb; when it was created. God set its limits. You shall come this far and no further. This is where your proud waves halt. There is a strength and majesty of the sea, but God is above that. Or, starting in 38:12: "Have you ever given orders to the morning or shown the dawn its place, that it might take the earth by the edges and shake the wicked out of it?"

The Light

This section of chapter 38, v12-15, is interesting because God speaks of the wicked and it has to do with light. This is not just day and night—it is partly that (where were you when God made those things)—but it is also this: the light shines on the wicked and exposes them. So now we have a light in another sense. I suppose the thief does not want physical light shining on him; he wants to do things in the dark; but he also does not want the light of the word of God shining on him and exposing his deeds for darkness. We get that in verses 13 and 15: "The wicked are denied their light." And here we have parallels with Genesis 1 and John 1. Think about how God is proceeding. God alone is eternal, God is the creator of even the most powerful things, God is the creator of light, and it is the light that exposes the wicked. "Those lost in darkness have seen a great light" (Is 9:2). Or think of how light is spoken of in Luke 1, the light coming for the Gentiles. And that light in John 1. We can ask, is this allegorical, bringing it in? Are we staying close to the text? Well, again, if it had not mentioned the wicked, this would be just about the day and night in creation. But here we have a specific mention of a light that is exposing the wicked and bringing their pride to nothing, breaking their arm. God does that. God rules, not just over creation; he rules providentially and morally. He is aware of the wicked. He brings them to an end. So this is not only a physical rule that is being described in these chapters, and that should work the fear of God in us. God rules over the wicked.

Death

Then in 38:16, there is an interesting connection with how God moves from the wicked to this next section: "The deep springs of the earth, the recesses of the deep." So there is this image of the depths of water, those ones that unleashed a flood. And the description continues to deep, secret places of the earth. But then it gets connected up to the gates of death. "Have the gates of death been shown to you? Have you seen the gates of the shadow of death? Have you comprehended the vast expanse of the earth? Tell me if you know all this" (v17-18). So that is an interesting move: from the wicked, to now God's rule over the imposition of death on the world. God is in charge of that as well. And that is a mystery people have wanted to solve. When will it happen and what will happen? We have some of the notable religious texts of the world about that: the Egyptian Book of the Dead; the Tibetan Book of the Dead, which will give a person detailed descriptions of what is going to happen to their soul as it leaves their body. People speculate about that. These are the mysteries they don't know, but God knows and God determined it. And death has that purpose. It is imposed after moral evil (wickedness) as a call back to stop and think about self-deception and self-justification. As we go through this, we have our knowledge of general revelation in place and our knowledge of Genesis in place. We don't just come to this as if we are newborn babes and know nothing. And we think, oh, this is Hades. In the previous section, God was talking about Sidon, and now he is talking about Hades. And this is just borrowed from the Greeks. No, absolutely not. Block that. We already have blocked that because Job is a theist who knows God the creator. Do we know the paths to the place of death? What is the outcome of the wicked? The purpose of death is a callback.

Surely You Know

38:19: "What about the way to the abode of light, and where does darkness reside? Can you put them in their places? Do you know the paths of their dwellings? Surely you know, for you were already born. You have lived so many years." What do we think about this? Is God allowed these rebuttals? Do we think of God as a kind of computer, and he would give us an answer like this and have no inflection and nothing besides the facts? Or can God put it to us the way we tried putting it to him? Soon we'll look at the things that Job had said. You are so old, Job. And even if we were so old, our time in life is so uncertain and feeble and short. Would Methuselah agree, let alone the rest of us? Do we think we can know where these things came from? That is a display of impiety toward God. Job should be ashamed of himself. And God does put it this way to Job: you've been there, Job, you've lived so many years. "Have you entered the storehouse of the snow?" Here we have the weather and the power of the weather. "For which I reserve for times of trouble, for days of war and battle" (v22-23). So, hail, snow and then war and battles between humans, and God's work in that. The winds. He cuts a channel for torrents of rain; satisfies a desolate wasteland. It gives a number of contrasts: wetland/desert, dry/rain. God is in charge of all these things.

Perfect Knowledge

For us, polytheism is not very real. God's questions are a direct shot to destroy that belief system. But it is not simply that, but also the idea that somehow there are gods that rule over certain spheres of human life, and even then, the gods are born and are inserted into it. They do their best to control those things, but they often fail in the mythologies. This, however, is God the creator over all things, who made all of else.

Could we doubt God's knowledge of them? God created them ex nihilo. Do we think God does not know? That is where we get perfect power and perfect knowledge together. God gave the created things natures. Do we think he does not care? How ridiculous that is. And God rules over all of these things that happen. These are questions to reflect on.

Again, what about the God of the gaps? Someone can say, "Okay, ancient people did not know where rain came from, but I know. There is the evaporation cycle and I have a handout from my fourth-grade teacher. The ocean evaporates and goes into the clouds, which get too much liquid, then go over land and the rain falls. So, Job did not know, but we know." Do we think that is satisfying? We have filled in the gaps. We don't need Zeus, we don't need Baal, we don't need God, the creator of all things. I have heard about different gods from polytheists, and this one I have heard from atheists. We have figured out these things. No. We haven't even come close to figuring them out. And on top of that, God isn't asking for mechanical knowledge alone. Even if we were to figure them out in some mechanical way, we don't have control over them. And even if we somehow did get some limited control—we can fly over a cloud and drop some dust into it and that makes it rain—it is still such limited abilities. It is pathetic in comparison to God.

The next section, 38:31: "Can you bind the beautiful Pleiades?" I went for a walk with my wife and we saw Orion there in the sky above us. Can we loose the cords of Orion? It was beautiful to see that and think about this. These constellations and their seasons. Lead out the Bear with its cubs. Do we know the laws of the heavens? Can we set up God's dominion over earth? So someone could say, "Yes, we figured these things out." We may have not figured it out, but either way is that answering it? Has any astronomer answered these questions? I know Kepler was a pious man and never would have said such a thing. But someone could take

Kepler's laws and say, yes, we figured out the rotation from these laws.

"Or raise your voice to the clouds?" (v34). It is interesting again that God goes through the laws of the heavens. The foundation of all things and the laws of things governing them. And even if we knew them, which we should, they are not ends in themselves. They reveal who God the creator is. Did we stop there? That is from John 1. Although they claimed to know the creation, they did not know the Logos. Those who study biology or astronomy or astrology don't know the God who made it.

That is our goal in doing this work of meditating on God's servant Job. "Or can you raise your voice to the clouds and cover yourself with a flood of water, or send the lightning bolts on their way?" (v35). This is how associative thinking works in allegoricalism. It is ridiculous. Well, Baal throws lightning bolts and Yahweh here says he does too, so this is Israel's Baal. Associative thinking—we need to be aware of that in many levels as we read scripture. We read something we think is relevant to some other passage because it says something similar, and then we combine them and miss the meaning of both. Associative thinking, which is where we end up getting allegoricalism. Now God gets to something very key here, in verse 36: "Who endowed the heart with wisdom or gave understanding to the mind? Who has the wisdom to count the clouds?" Wisdom, understanding. God created these physical things; he created the human mind, which can understand them and have wisdom. And that tells us that God has understanding and God's not just a force like gravity or something. God can do these things. Did you do these things, Job? Did you have understanding?

Specific Creatures

In 38:39 God switches into a theme that continues throughout the rest of chapter 39, switching to specific animals. The lion here: "Do you hunt the prey for the lioness and satisfy the hunger of lions when they crouch in their dens and lie in wait in a thicket?" (see also psalm 34:10) The lion. I don't know how much connection we have with this animal; there are some mountain lions around us, but this lion is larger and even more ferocious. And the lioness, the hunter. How would we do with the lion? Is it more terrifying than other creatures, than the grizzly bear? The grizzly bear would be bad, too, if we meet it out in the wild—he is hungry. What would we do? Lay down and play dead? Who came up with that idea? The grizzly bears, right? They don't want to have to chase us, so they came up with the idea: hey, if you ever meet one of us, just play dead. Just make it easy on all of us. It will be better that way. But the lion's even faster than the grizzly.

Then God gets to the raven. Psalm 147 mentions ravens too. This is a way of connecting the wisdom literature in seeing what is taught from creation about wisdom. And the Psalms affirm all these same things about wisdom. And then guess what? In Matthew 6:26, God "cares for the birds of the air. Do you not think he also cares for you?" How could Job have come to this place of questioning if God cares for him? Of course, God loves Job. He cares for the ravens, and when their young cry out, he gives them food. And you thought that God does not care for you, Job? Well—look how mean he is been. And look what I have gone through. Well then, you've not seen your condition and what God is doing for you in this. And that is actually the depth of the love of God. The great mercy of God is being shown to you.

Chapter 39: what about the mountain goats that give birth? Again, we can imagine some zoologist saying, "Yes, we have actually set up cameras and we have proof of how the mountain goats give birth." That is not the point here. Going from the ferocious lion now to the fawn, the doe, and the mountain goat. Their young thrive and grow strong in the wild. They leave and do not return.

And then 39:5: God points to this wild donkey who rejoices in his freedom. Who untied his rope? Who gave it this instinct for freedom? We do have wild donkey herds here around Lake Pleasant. Sometimes I'll see them out there. We couldn't tame them if we wanted to. Where do they get that instinct for freedom? They live out away from civilization, on the salt flats, away from it all. Maybe they move there to preserve that freedom. And God finds joy in seeing this. This donkey laughs at the commotion in the town, the other animals that have been captured and tamed and contribute to that commotion in the town. The donkey sees that and says, look at them, I am free still; I am in the country. Who made it that way? Then the wild ox: "Can it consent to serve you?" (v9a). The wild ox is a very powerful brute—if someone asks him to serve them, will he do it? "Will he stay by your manger at night? Can you hold him in the furrow with a harness? Can you rely on him for his great strength? Will you leave your heavy work to him?" (v9b-11)

We get these different creatures and their attributes, and this is reminiscent of Adam in the Garden. God is calling us back to that work of knowing him through dominion. Did you name the creatures? And he went from those big pieces of creation, the foundation of all things, light and darkness, and even the wicked—and he asks now, did you name the creatures? Here are some examples. Have you noticed these things? That was the first thing Adam was asked to do. That was the beginning of his work. God is calling back to that. Have you done that, Job?

What about the ostrich in 39:13? I hear ostrich lovers got a little upset here. They say God is getting it wrong; the ostrich is actually a very caring parent, both the male and female ostrich take care of their eggs, not just the female. So, what does this mean, "it leaves it there"? Well, that does not negate the point here. A flightless bird leaving it in the sand in a less safe way, where it is easily trampled by others. And people have noticed that about the ostrich treating her young harshly. Verse 17: God does not give her wisdom of a kind, the shrewdness of the lion, but when she spreads her feathers to run, she laughs at the horse and the rider. If someone has ever seen the beauty of the ostrich and the speed of the ostrich, its feathers—there is a kind of glory to this otherwise somewhat awkward creature. And the speed of the ostrich. We could have ostrich races, laughing at both the horse and the rider. There is some joy here, both God in the creation and in the creation itself. Joy in the powers endued by God. Have we seen that? Have we observed that? Have we reduced nature to a feat of strength to be conquered? Have we reduced nature to a pragmatic thing to be used? Or do we see it as a revelation of God, the wisdom of God making the nature of things?

And now the horse, who gets quite a section. Horse lovers love this section. The strength of the horse, the neck with a flowing mane. "Did you make him leap like a locust, striking terror with his proud snorting? He paws fiercely, rejoicing in his strength and charging into the fray." We couldn't get an ostrich to do that. The way the horse goes into battle. And the ox is much too slow, but the horse rushes in there, and there is a beauty of a trained war horse. Alexander the Great tamed his horse, and that is when his father knew that it was a war horse. Going into the fray of battle. He laughs at fear. He is afraid of nothing. We can imagine that—there are movies about it where they try to make realistic versions of that, and we see these sides with horses just hit each other. Someone might think to themselves; "I don't want to do that; what's the horse doing?" The horse running into that, laughing at fear, afraid of nothing. It does not shy away from the sword. The implication here is that there have been some battles with horses in Job's time. Humans haven't been having a peaceful time this whole time, even though the book of Job is an early part of human history. But there are horses being used for that and they can be used in a unique way that the other animals so far couldn't. I like this in 39:24: "With frenzied excitement he eats up the ground, and he cannot stand still when the trumpet sounds." Eagerness to get into battle. "At the blast of the trumpet he snorts, Aha! He catches the scent of battle from afar, the shout of the commanders and the battle cry." What a creature. What a description of this one. Did you make him, Job? Did you create the nature of things? Have you named him as you should have? Have you understood him?

And then 39:26: "Does the hawk take flight by your wisdom?" God is coming back to the theme of wisdom and understanding. Do you understand, Job? Do you have wisdom? Did you give it wisdom? God is the creator of the nature of things. That is in the sense in which God is good. God determined their natures, and that is including human nature. What about the hawk and its wisdom? Think about how hard it is for us. If someone just gave me a big hanger with a lot of parts and he said, that is all the parts you need for a Boeing—make one. What? I don't know what to do. Maybe they gave me a team of guys and I still would not know what to do. It is very difficult. And that is not anywhere close to a hawk. And the ease with which a hawk can fly. There is a family of Harris Hawks near my house; I love watching them and the ease with which they can do things, and they make it look so simple and so beautiful. He spreads his wings.

How about the eagle? We have falcon, hawk, and eagle in terms of altitude. An eagle can get up there in altitude and soar. "He dwells on the cliff, he stays there at night. From there he seeks out his food. His young ones feast on blood, and where the slain are, there he is." That is an interesting ending out of chapter 39. Natural evil is here. God is affirming that and talking about the ravens. But then here especially, things die and God's in charge of that also. It is very different than saying it is a "circle of life." Remember that movie where the monkey's holding up a baby lion, and I guess he is going to sacrifice the baby lion to the animals or something and chuck it over the cliff? Is that what it was? And they are all rejoicing because they want to see the lion killed finally? And it is all a circle of life? This isn't that. This is God ruling over all, including natural evil. This comes back to Satan at the beginning. The powers within the creation are all under God, even powers that seem destructive. Whether it is Satan, or the ocean that is sometimes thought of as chaos. Humans have no control over it, compared to the land, which is firm. God is in charge of all those things.

What Job Said about God

Where does Job fit into this? There is a pause now. "The Lord said to Job, 'Will the one who contends with the Almighty correct him?'" (40:2). Job had said in chapter 9, "God overthrows the structures of the earth," in contrast to God saying, "I laid the foundations of the earth." In chapters 3 and 7, Job says, "God hedges in the way of mortals and muzzles Job as if it were the sea." And now God says he is the one who creates the sea and sets its limits and calls it proud. Chapter 9 again: Job said, "God smiles over the design of the wicked and hands over the earth to them." Job said that about God. God says no—he shines a light on the wicked so that their pride is destroyed. Job said Sheol is the realm that is free from the cruel hand of God. Job said that about God. And here God says, no, he created those things. Do you know where death is, Job? The gate of death? God created that. God imposed death for a purpose. How could Job have said that?

Job sought to remove the day and night of the origins of his life. He said, I wish I'd never been born, that the light never shined on me. Job also said God's design is to manipulate the weather for his own destructive ends in chapter 12. Job said that about God. Job said, "God employs his eternal wisdom to create chaos on earth." He said in chapter 10 that God hunts him like a lion. So again, God goes back to the lions. We can set this up very well to show God's responses to these things. So if we were paying attention to what Job says, we'll be able to see why God is responding the way he is. Why is God bringing up lions? Job had said God hunts him like a lion and does not heed his cry. And God then compares the lions, and says, I heed the cry of the baby ravens. Job said, "God fixes the brief lifespan of mortals to oppress them." And here God says, "I've set the times of the living creatures for their benefit." Job said, the place of freedom is Sheol, far from God's oppressive voice, and God cannot be trusted to answer my cry, and God is arbitrary in the way he allocates portions of fate. If only God restrained his terror, life would be fair and a trial with him would be possible. He said the eye of God spies on mortals as if God's looking on things to get people.

This is what Job added to his account. When I said self-deception and self-justification, this is what Job has said of God. So, we can both love our brother Job and agree with Elihu: these things are not right. And that is what God is responding to now. He is just done that; he just addressed all of these in chapters 38 and 39.

Job answers at this point and says to the Lord, to Yahweh, "I am unworthy. How can I reply to you? I put my hand over my mouth. I spoke once, but I have no answer; twice, but I will say no more" (40:4-5). An apology? No. This isn't far enough yet. It does not end there. The Lord spoke to Job out of the storm in the next verse: "I will question you and you will answer me." It is not enough to be quiet, Job. You need to repent of what you've said. And he hasn't gotten there yet. Job certainly could have at this point; he could have repented after Elihu spoke. He was silent after Elihu and he repeats that here—I am silent. We might think, well, it is going far enough, don't press it too hard. No, we need to get forgiveness and cleansing.

Now he goes into chapter 40. God says in verse 8, "Would you discredit my justice? Would you condemn me to justify yourself?" That is what Job added. When this trial started, God's servant Job still needed to go further. But then after that, he added these incorrect things about God. He justified himself at the expense of God. "Do you have an arm like God's, or can your voice thunder like his? Then adorn yourself with glory and splendor and clothe yourself in honor and majesty. Unleash the fury of your wrath. Look at every proud man and bring him low. Look at every proud man and humble him. Crush the wicked where they stand. Bury them all in the dust together, shroud their faces in the grave. Then I myself will admit to you that your own right hand can save you" (40:14). What a challenge from God to humble Job.

Repentance

But that is not the end. God wants repentance in the inward parts—we can think of Psalm 51. So this view that God is just crushing Job, he is humbling him, he is putting him in his place—no. God says he wants to humble the proud and he wants to crush the wicked. God is working in his providence redemptively, with each of us as he needs to, in his perfect wisdom. And Christ draws our attention to that again in Matthew 6: if he cares for the grass of the field and he cares for the birds, do you not think he cares for you? It is atheism to say "no, God doesn't. Somehow I have missed out; somehow God overlooked me in his infinity and he forgot about me." Job is going to need to go further. That is why chapter 42 needs to be looked at in depth. But we need to see how God brings him to that.

God's purpose in these chapters illustrates exactly what is needed to get someone's attention. What does it take to get our attention, our focus? We will easily dismiss sin. It is not a big deal, who cares, what does it matter to God, he is distant. Some may say, why does

God answer this way? God, in his perfection, is showing us that this is what it takes to get our attention. Not simply to humble us and say, ok, alright—uncle—you are stronger than me; but to get us to see what sin is. And that is why it is such a great connection even back to the beginning of our work in the Garden, naming the creation. Did we see that creation is revelation, and do we find our joy in knowing God?

Behemoth and Leviathan

God has been asking questions about the creation and this continues with these two creatures. There is no shift here to occult powers or polytheistic deities. The context from general revelation rules these out before we get to the text. And it is a good example of how those who miss general revelation will also misunderstand the text. We can know from general revelation that the occult and polytheism are false. We do not need God to tell us that He has control over false gods. The readers at that time had access to the same general revelation.

In the last part of chapter 40 and then in 41, God turns his attention to two creatures: Behemoth and Leviathan. I have spent some considerable time thinking about what these creatures are. As I read other commentaries there are generally three options: a currently living natural creature, an extinct but natural creature, or a supernatural creature. I am ruling out the supernatural one because this whole thing is about creation, as opposed to saying this is the same story of Horus fighting Set. Leviathan is Set, God is Horus and it is the same story. Or Baal fighting the many-headed sea monster. No, that is allegoricalism, associative thinking. Those involve a monster, this involves a monster; therefore, it is the same story. No. That would be allegorical in the sense that we are bringing in some foreign context—Canaanite, Egyptian, and Greek context—to a theistic text. They say this is Satan or Death since such is the case in Canaanite literature. So, I am ruling that one out. My argument: these two creatures are part of the created world. The Canaanite deities aren't real and so aren't part of the created world. Nor are these creatures spiritual beings or states of being, as the emphasis here in Job is on how the creation reveals God the Creator. When someone is interpreting Job, and doesn't themselves know about the clarity of general revelation, they will miss it in what God says here as well and even being in something contrary to the Biblical worldview.

Some say that the author of Job, or the audience of Job, would have believed the truth of the Canaanite type stories. This is contrary to what we know both from general revelation and from Genesis 1-3. The assertion that the audience of Job was benighted because they lived in the ancient world has no merit. They had access to the same general revelation of God's eternal power and divine nature as we do. There is no basis for claiming they believed Canaanite type accounts any more than claiming that believers today accept unbelieving accounts. And this is especially true of the author of Job. But we know for certain that the greatest creatures reveal the works of their Creator so this is the understanding of this text that fits all we know, and the other understanding is contrary to what we know. This is a good example of how to apply contextual interpretation in contrast either to literalism or allegoricalism.

These are describing some very grand creatures which aren't with us anymore. This isn't like the hippopotamus or the crocodile. But they are parts of the creation. I know people like to look into dinosaurs, and we see how massive these are. What must it have been like to be around such a creature? That is why the 1993 Jurassic Park movie has the place it does, because it gave the first kind of realism where people are saying, wow, look at what that would be like. So we read these descriptions and the power in them. It is describing these great pieces of creation that humans can barely get involved with. It says, "You'll regret the day you tried." And God made them; God's in charge of them. Can you do these things, Job? No. Yet God made them from nothing.

In 40:19, of the Behemoth, God says, "He ranks first among the works of God, yet his maker can approach him with his sword." First among the creatures of God. Sometimes this is said to be the hippopotamus and alligator. I do not think the descriptions fit that close enough. Can anyone capture this one by the eyes or track him and pierce his nose? The behemoth. And in chapter 41, there is an even longer description of Leviathan. "Can you pull in the Leviathan with a fishhook or tie down his tongue with a rope? Can you put a cord through his nose or pierce his jaw with a hook?" (41:2). I was thinking about stories we have of that, like Ahab going after Moby Dick, and long descriptions in that book of hunting whales and all that it is like, and those that were in charge of throwing the harpoon and the power they had to have, and how many harpoons you have to get into the creature, and how it can still pull the entire boat with it. And those are less than Leviathan. What would it be like to get involved with these creatures? Can you make him a pet like a bird and put him on a leash, or barter for him and divide him up among the merchants? (41:5). And in verse 7, "Can you fill his hide with harpoons or his head with fishing spears? If you lay a hand on him, you'll remember the struggle and never do it again." So, what of this creature? We do not have any hope of subduing him—it would take such a struggle. Then in the next section God begins to speak about the fire that is in him. "Firebrands stream from his mouth. Sparks of fire shoot out. Smoke pours from his nostrils as from a boiling pot over a fire of reeds. His breath sets coal ablaze, and flames dart from his mouth. The strength that resides in his neck" (41:19-22). What a creature that God made here. And this is after building up through many creatures, each of which had their own majesty. Lion, raven, goat, ostrich. Different and majestic.

Seeing God

What do we make of this description? Have we studied creation? Have we named the creation? Have we seen the glory of God displayed in the creation? Have we found our meaning in that? I have been struck recently by how many of the traditionalists are talking about the beatific vision. When we die, we will see Christ, or at the resurrection, we' will see Christ. And that is true. But what is this "seeing" Christ? What is it to see God? Many people saw Christ in his earthly ministry and did not understand. We might say, well, but this will be the resurrected body. Peter saw the transformed, transfigured body of Christ and did not understand. So, one kind of beatific vision is an attempt to get some vision of God apart from his creation. This beatific vision is the attempt to get to God apart from the Word of God that makes God known. It is enough to see him in another sense of understanding him, and that is what Job is being pointed to. Did you see God, Job? Did you find your joy in knowing God? That was the issue from the beginning that Job was being brought to a greater understanding of. But then he compounded it with self-deception and self-justification, going so far as to say about God these things we have read. And we can see now why Elihu would be riled up and angry. *We* should have been angry when we heard things like that about God. And God is responding now to Job. What does it take to get our attention and our focus? What does it take to see the glory of God displayed in the creation, to find our highest good in that?

Getting to Root Sin

Here's how we know Job needed to go further. Remember what Job said he had wanted out of life, followed by the famous "but now." The things preceding that were very natural things. They weren't necessarily wrong. It is not as if he wanted to live off drug money. Job wanted very natural things that anybody would want as they grow up. I'd like to have a nice job that has a sufficient income to take care of a little family and raise them. Wouldn't it be nice? And we find our contentment in these things. We do not find our contentment in knowing God. That is what we saw Job describing for his sense of what the good life is. But he needs to go further, and God in his mercy is teaching Job to go further. Then Job turns around and accuses God of not caring, instead of seeing this as the love of God.

How many times has that happened to us under authority? If we come under authority, our immediate response is, they are wrong. I am right and I'll defend myself. And sometimes human authority is wrong. So, it is very different than God, who's not wrong. But if we can do it to God, how much more do we expect to do it to human authority as well? We would use that justification even more. "Well, you are just a human." But there is legitimate authority in the world. And what should be somewhat dumbfounding, although not really, because it should remind us about the human condition, is that Job did accuse God of not caring and we are all doing that about God. This is our condition before God—we have deceived ourselves about our condition.

We should wonder about that, and we can take that application here: how has God spoken? Why did God choose to speak this way to Job, for all of us? Job is for all of us: "Have you considered God's servant Job?" Job needs to come to know himself. He does not have self-knowledge. And that was revealed through these trials. Because of that the trials are a good thing, something to rejoice in, because they bring this out in us and in Job. What Job did, he did ignorantly and out of unbelief. Remember when Paul says that? Perhaps one of the greatest intellects in human history, and that very talent was turned on its head and used to try to eradicate the early church. And Paul summarizes it by saying, what I did, I did ignorantly, out of unbelief. God's exposing the same thing about Job. Do you understand, Job? Then show me that you understand. Are you ignorant of things you should know? That ignorance leads to these awful things that you've said.

We need to repent of our failure to know what we should, and then our compounding that with self-deception and self-justification. It is not enough to be silent and to say we won't speak anymore. We could say that—we could say, "every time I talk, I get into trouble. I am just going to be quiet." That was Job there at the end of chapter 39. God's going to take Job further than that. He is going to say "No, you actually need to go further and repent of these things." We must believe that God is, and that he is the rewarder of those who diligently seek him. And this is what it takes to get us to pay attention. We can't complain about how much it takes to get us to pay attention. Isn't that ironic? Because the solution to those trials is, pay attention. So, God has successfully responded to Job in exactly the way we would expect—the most masterful way. Yahweh.

There is a mastery that is used later in history, when the Word of God incarnate is responding to the Pharisees. We have seen that in the Bible. But as we have looked at this section of Job, we are looking at something that is unique. God is speaking. We consider the words of God and can ask ourselves, have I found my joy in knowing God? Do I come to God knowing that he is and that he is the rewarder of those who diligently seek him? Incidentally, those go together—that God *is*. That is the name "Yahweh." Only God is eternal, and we can derive much from the nature of God if we know those things. It is not simply, oh yeah, there is some guy named God. We must know that God is, and that he rewards those who diligently seek him, because that is the break that the biblical atheist tries to make: God is distant. He does not care about us. He is in his heavens, and we are down here. And there, Paul is combining those together. What that reward is: knowing God himself is a reward. So we can be thankful to God for these chapters, for getting our attention and praying that we would pay attention and be focused and benefit from what God's servant Job is going through. We now see why we need special focus on just Job's answer. We need to look at some details of Job and his friends and what repentance is, what Job illustrates. All that time and suffering requires more attention than just throwing on at the last second that Job repented.

Job Part Seven

Now My Eyes See You

42:5-6
My ears had heard of you but now my eyes have seen you. Therefore I despise myself and repent in dust and ashes.

Ecclesiastes 7:8: "The end of a matter is better than its beginning, and patience is better than pride." The end of a matter is better than its beginning. And we come now to the end of the book of Job and the end of this story. Job 42 is the shortest section we have looked at. We are at the height, the peak of the action in the book. It took that long narrative buildup to get here. And it made me wonder, do people have a favorite story that they like to watch over and over, or maybe a favorite book they like to read over and over? People do that sometimes; they can put a movie on auto replay. And they know what's going to happen, they already know the outcome, the resolution; there is not anything new, there is no surprises—especially at that point. Maybe if they've watched it the second or third time, they might say, "Oh, I saw some new things." But it gets to a point with a favorite story where they say "Yeah, I know what's going to happen," and there is almost a kind of comfort in it. And so as we are looking at Job, it might be fun to contrast and think about what favorite stories we do that with. "Oh, good—the Ring did get thrown into the lava; I was worried. Oh good—the torpedo did go down the shaft and blow up the Death Star." So we come to the end of the story of Job and we want to know what's going to happen.

For those who read through the Bible in a year, I know that they have already come to the end. They know what happens. And there is something to that; we are coming to this conclusion, pressing us to the point of Job's repentance, from which comes the resolution of the conflicts and the conclusion of the matter with each of the main characters. But did we catch what happens or have we missed it in our many readings? Did we miss repentance from root sin? And have we repented of the root sin of not seeing what is clear about God in the works of God?

Here we have the biblical hero. We can see what the hero quest is, the hero narrative, and see the pagan idolatrous hero narrative and contrast it with the biblical one. At the very beginning of all of this, early on (this is sometime before the law of Moses, after Babel), we have this story—what does God expect of a hero? What does a biblical hero look like? A godly hero? This is at a very early point in human history. We are going to be shown that; we are to have considered that in all the ages since then. To have reflected on God's servant Job. Even now, to this very point, the thing of which Job repents is what the church, what each of us, needs to repent of now. We consider the various heroes in our favorite stories, the types of personalities they represent, and we'll see how far the unbeliever gets in knowing what makes a hero.

What brings Job through this trial? How does he slay the dragon? That is not only a metaphor for paying close attention. It is been a terrible conflict—terrible in the sense of fearful. That is not meant merely in terms of the negative thing. It has been a fearful conflict, one which should have produced in us the fear of the Lord when we observe these wise men at odds with each other. All of those involved were reputed for their wisdom. And they are at great odds with each other and they've come short. That is fearful and dreadful, isn't it? And we saw how they spoke to Job, and we saw how far Job was pressed and what he was saying. And then we saw him asking for a mediator, asking to try his case before God, and then God speaks to him. So, it is not just that Job goes through terrible physical suffering, and we say to ourselves, oh, I hope I'll never go through that. That is for Job. And probably we won't to the degree to which Job went through it. But it isn't really just that. Because we could have the suffering Olympics and see who suffered the most. But that is not the point of the suffering in Job; the point comes out especially in the existential suffering and struggle, the torment caused by his friends and their baseless accusations. The comforters of Job. With comforters like that, who needs enemies? Each of these came in with a reputation for wisdom, and they also had claims to wisdom. I am going to quote some of what they said and see how it comes back on them. And they cause more suffering for Job in their behavior. So, we wonder, what will become of them? One should not presume to be a teacher if they don't know the basic things.

Satan and the Accusation

What will happen to these friends? Remember to think about Satan and how he put all this into motion with his accusation of Job. "Job only loves God for what he gets." What does that say about Job, and what does that say about God? We are going to think back on Satan as well. But Job's trial has been guided by God this whole time. We don't want to give Satan the credit for having started it off, because God asked, "Have you considered my servant Job?" (1:8). And he never let go of that servant all the way until the end. The excellence of God's servant Job is displayed. God returns that endearing title to Job in this ending chapter: my servant Job. Satan thought one thing, and he was shown to be badly mistaken. And it wasn't simply a defeat; it was a glorious defeat for all the ages to see. That is why I talked slaying that dragon. Remember the hero, Beowulf, the monsters. Here we have Satan's accusations brought back on him and the glory of God displayed in his servant Job. The perfect hand of God is at work in this whole process. This is the glory that comes out in the excellence of Job in repentance from root sin. And we can't let that phrase become an empty saying, a platitude—oh yeah, repentance from root sin—we want to capture the depth of that and hold onto it and see it in the text.

Answering God

God did not stop halfway. Beginning in chapter 38, God continues. There is a revelation, there is forgiveness, and there is cleansing. In 38:2-3 God says, "Who is this that darkens my counsel with words without knowledge? Brace yourself like a man and I will question you and you shall answer me." How would we like to be asked that by God? Prepare to answer me. Well, if it were out of the blue, that is one thing. Job had asked for this—he wanted to try his case. What do we think is going to happen if we ask to try our case? Words without knowledge. Brace yourself like a man. Do we want an account? That is something essential to being a human. We want to give an account of ourselves. But then it goes on here in 40:6-7: "Then the Lord spoke to Job out of the storm. Brace yourself like a man; I will question you and you shall answer me." That is the second time. Because in the beginning of chapter 40, we have the first response of Job to God: will the one who contends with the Almighty correct him? Let him who accuses God answer him (40:2). And Job says, "I am unworthy. How can I reply to you? I put my hand over my mouth. I spoke once, but I have no answer; twice, but I will say no more."

So here we have at the beginning of chapter 40 some recognition of God's omnipotence. We already saw that earlier in the text as well; and Job remained silent. But God does not stop there. That is not where Job—and we—need to get to. Job has not repented of what happened yet. So, God continued in chapter 40 and 41. It is almost as if someone might acknowledge a mistake—and there are reasons that people might acknowledge a mistake, but they are not repenting yet; they are not getting through to it. So part of what we are seeing here is what is needed to get us to see the depth of our sin and repent of that. We have four chapters in God's response to Job. The first two get us only to where Job confesses a mistake, but he hasn't yet repented. The second two bring us to where we are at now.

Four Views

I mention the shortcomings in these solutions because I have categorized the four common responses or views of what goes on in Job in chapter 42, as I am looking at various commentaries. Some commentaries show someone could read Job and even claim to be reflecting on it, yet miss what is happening in the works of God and the repentance of Job. One says that Job comes to recognize the omnipotence of God. And he confesses, yes, God, you are omnipotent. Now, that is what he essentially did in chapter 40, and he had also said things earlier that show he knows that God is omnipotent. This confession from Job is not some new startling thing and so it is no basis for repentance. So that is not a successful view.

Another view is that Job comes to recognize the rule of God and the details of the world in a new way, one he hadn't thought of before. Maybe that is inching closer, but it is still not getting to root sin, and Job and his friends had all talked about the work of God in creation. They still need to repent of root sin.

The third one recognizes the power of God, and God is a kind of irrational tyrant that has to be appeased. This commentary takes Job's repentance as tongue in cheek. That is a view that is been out there for a while, but there is a recent commentary about that as well. It says Job is saying, I repent to appease God, who then is apparently easy to fool, and he takes the bait and is fooled. And that comes badly short.

The fourth one says that the word "repent" means "turn from God." I repent *of* you. At the end, Job turns away altogether from God because God is flexing his muscles and there is nothing in the answer that makes suffering worth it, and there is no justification for the suffering Job has gone through.

I have also mentioned Carl Jung—that might make you want to go read Carl Jung instead and his Gnosticism to interpret Job. So, these commentaries aren't getting it; they are not getting to the point of it. Why? What happened? How could they miss the book of Job? Well, I think they are not seeing this distinction between root and fruit sin, and they are not seeing the clarity of general revelation themselves. They can't then say Job should repent of something of which they aren't even aware. They are in that same place of Job, or perhaps as Job's accusers. So we are going to see how God completes the work that he began. He does not stop with Job in chapter 40. We get to chapter 42. And all of this is because God loved Job and God is revealing something about Job, about redemption, and about God himself—his nature, his justice and his mercy. And even when it might have appeared that Job had faltered, this was only part of the purpose God had in bringing out what was still in Job that needed to be cleansed. Here is both repentance and cleansing. What does it take to cleanse us from sin? The sin was there, but so is the final repentance. And we did not see this in the same way in his friends, which I will talk about later.

The Problem

From the very beginning, we have been wrestling with this question of suffering. Why do we suffer? How do we make sense of it? All have suffered; even the very young have suffered. And we want to make sense of it. There is a kind of practical solution, getting over our suffering—find out what caused it, and cure it. We want to have some control over it. Don't shake hands anymore; just do fist bumps—that will prevent the virus. But it does not help us understand the meaning of why it happened in the first place. That is what the book of Job has helped us with. Why is the world managed the way it is? Is it unfair? Does God know what he is doing? How can we make sense of it? How can we find meaning in the world? If we cannot find meaning, it would be better not to have been born. We don't want just generalities; we want to get down into particulars. That is what platitudes are: nice sayings that sound good. "Hey, you should lead the examined life." How do we apply that? What are the particularities of that? How do we get down to this? "You should seek meaning." Well, gee, thanks for the insights. How do we get down to that? That is why we got these details in Job's life, and now it is on each of us to apply that in our own life as well. How do I make sense of my own life and my situation? So, what are the particulars of Job's repentance in this chapter?

Seven Final Pieces

I have chapter 42 roughly divided into seven pieces: 1. Job's affirmation of God; 2. Job's response to God's questions and confession; 3. What God said and how Job responds to it; 4. His three friends and God's anger at them/what happens with them, and that name returns; 5. "My servant Job"—offerings and prayer are part of that; 6. Then his restoration, family and friends coming; 7. Then the latter part of his life and his vindication, ending with the generations of Job and a life full of years and how we should take that. The perfect ending and how we might think about that applying to us.

Remember some of the things Job had said about God: God overthrowing the structures of the earth, hedging in the way of mortals, muzzling Job as if he were the sea, smiling on the design of those who seem to be wicked, and handing the earth over to them. Sheol is a realm that is free from the hand of God, a potential refuge from his anger. Job wanted to remove the day of his birth from the calendar. He had talked about God's use of the weather, God employing his wisdom toward ends that seem hard to understand on earth, God hunting Job like a lion, and not heeding his cry. God fixing the brief span of mortals to oppress them, Job saying the place of freedom is death, far from God's oppressive voice. God cannot be trusted to answer Job's cry, God appears to be arbitrary in the way he apportions fate, etc. There are a few more here, but the idea of such solutions is getting to the purpose of how God rules in life. Because when we see these kinds of solutions, we see that some of those are part of what God does. They are partial answers. God does use natural evil to restrain the wicked, but God does sometimes allow there to appear to be prosperity in the wicked because he is disciplining those he loves. So we can't stop with these accusations. And God asks him, would you justify yourself at my expense? So we know that Job has sinned, and this makes us wonder, what does it mean to be blameless? 40:2: "Will the one who contends with the Almighty correct him?" And verse 8: "Would you discredit my justice? Would you condemn me to justify yourself?"

These are not a full description of God and the working of God. These are why we need to see natural evil and the purpose of natural evil. If we come to the book without the clarity of general revelation, without the clarity of God's existence in place, we won't make any sense of it. I mentioned earlier that we are going to be putting Job in the context of the biblical worldview. That is different than putting it in the context of the archaeology of the day, or putting it in a certain linguistic context. We are putting in the context of the biblical worldview, that our highest good is in knowing God. What if we came to the book of Job and we did not think our highest good was in knowing God through all of his works? We'd end up in one of these sorry interpretations, right? That is a kind word for them. What if we came to the book of Job and we did not know that natural evil is a callback from moral evil, including self-deception and self-justification? We would not get very far. Natural evil as a call back from moral evil is partly what some of his friends were talking about when they were talking about the role of natural evil. But it is not just due to sin; it is getting through to self-deception, the ways we tell ourselves, "Things are okay; sin is not that big of a deal."

Sin and Death

"Sin won't lead to death." That is the original lie, as they call it. Do we believe that one? Then there is self-justification, defending ourselves to others. Those cycles are in the book and in the arguments between Job and his friends. What if we came to the book of Job and did not have a distinction between fruit and root sin? If we just thought of sin at the fruit level? We'd have a hard time making sense of what it means to say Job is blameless. That is easily understood once we make those distinctions: blameless before others, but ultimately having root sin that is the same as all men. So we don't want to let those distinctions become empty because of repetition, but rather we must understand the importance of them and their meaning. If we did not come to Job with these in mind, we'd fall into what even the secularists can affirm, that nature is great, that nature has lots of neat things to see and lots of design. But again, this does not make any sense for the rest of the book. Job and his friends had already talked about the works of God, so that is not what Job is about. Those interpretations should easily fall apart when we look at them.

Now I Know You

After God finished four chapters of questioning showing Job His handiwork, Job says to God, "I know that you can do all things. No plan of yours can be thwarted." He is affirming who God is after having this revelation. What is that "all things" Job refers to? I do not think it is simply an "all things" which he might have said earlier in the book. He is referring to all things, including this work in Job's life, which he hadn't seen before. Job's reference to "all things" can't simply be a repetition of something that he had already seen before; it must be something new, something deeper.

"You asked, 'Who is this that obscures my counsel without knowledge?' Surely, I spoke of things I did not understand, things too wonderful for me" (42:3). So here we have the beginning of Job's confession. "I thought I knew but I did not know. There were things that I did not understand." Now, that view of Job which says that he only just now has awe in the face of the mysterious, the numinous, does not fit this. One could try to force that there and say, "God is just beyond us. We can't know anything about God. That is what Job came to know. God is way beyond us. And it was our fault for trying to understand God, and we should remain silent.: No. That is what happened at the beginning of chapter 40. Job isn't there. That wasn't the end of it.

We went from 40 and now we are in 42. That is not what's happening, because Job goes on: "You said, 'Listen now, and I will speak. I will question you and you shall answer me.' My ears had heard of you." So Job restates what God said, "I will question you." God catechized Job. We may have heard of the Grand Inquisitor; that pales in comparison. How would we like that for the person giving our final exam? We might think about that, the first exam by the serpent: "Did God really say?" The final exam is what Job was asked by God. These are the things you should know, Job. I'll question you and you'll answer me. So now we get to the fullness of his repentance: "My ears had heard of you, but now my eyes have seen you. Therefore, I despise myself and repent in dust and ashes" (5-6).

Repent: Change Your Mind and Do Something About It

Notice when this repentance is occurring in the chapter. This is before Job is restored and cleansed. So we can't give some reading of Job and say, "well, of course he repents—he got everything back." No. And we can't say, "well, he knew he was going to get everything back." No, nothing in there tells us that at all. Job is still covered in boils, on an ash heap, with nothing. And he says these things in response to God because his understanding has changed. That is what it means when he says, "I repent." This is from the Latin, "to think again"; to rethink." I am thinking again, I have rethought my earlier position.

But that is not sufficient to capture repentance. The Greek and especially the Hebrew help us. The Greek is "to change your mind" and the Hebrew captures that: change your mind and do something about it—because one could rethink it and not do anything about it. I thought again, and I was doing the right thing in the first place. So it means rethink in the sense of "to change your mind." Specifically, here, Job is changing his mind about what? About God and God's actions. And about himself, realizing, "I was wrong about myself." Remember Job's concern for his integrity. That is something that was part of what God asked him: you try to preserve your integrity by impugning mine. Job had to rethink his view of himself and his integrity.

So what is he rethinking? What is he changing his mind on? Is it correct to say these are basic things, God and man, God and Job? He is rethinking these. These are the basics—Job is getting to the root level of his thinking. And it took God's catechizing, his guiding questions, to get Job there.

What will it take us to rethink those things about our life? How easy or hard is it to get us to stop and think? Sometimes some teachers will say, that would be a miracle. To rethink, to do it twice. If the student would just think for the first time, I'll be happy with that. To rethink and to change our mind. Will we be any different than Job? This is our example held up from this early time in history down to the present.

To see how Job has come to repent, we can compare what he said back in chapter 9. Earlier, Job had used this word: he said, I *despise* myself, or I *abhor* myself. He had used that word earlier in 9:21. "Although I am blameless," Job said, "I have no concern for myself. I despise my own life." The same word. Isn't that the same thing here? He despised himself before, and now he despises himself again. No, it is completely different here. "I am blameless." No repentance in that statement. "I have no concern for myself." Why not? Should not you at least be concerned for the good for yourself? "I despise my own life." That is where he gets to saying he would rather he had never been born. Have we ever felt that? I wonder if teenagers have said that. "I wish I were never born. I did not ask to be born." That is not getting to greater understanding or repentance, is it? That is a mistaken view about life and suffering. We could have, in pride, both an elevated, prideful view, and a devalued but still prideful view of the self-life. They are both wrong. So here Job says the same thing: now I abhor myself. The "abhor myself" has to be in relation to what he just said to God: "Now I see you. I did not before. That is why I abhor myself." Back in chapter 9, he was abhorring his lot in life, saying, if this is what life comes to, it is not worth it.

See the change in Job? That is what we have to understand in chapter 42. The change in Job: from earlier Job to present Job. That is the hero that we want to hold up. He got it. He grew in understanding. And when we see that excellence, will we jump up in our seat and clap? Look at Job! He did it. The repentance has to come in reference to, "Now I see you." And that is like our term for "see." We use that both physically and as a metaphor for understanding. It is the same thing here. And it can't mean physically seeing the non-physical. God spoke to Job out of the whirlwind, but we do not get any sense that he saw something called God. He saw a whirlwind. So, if we try to press it as physical seeing it won't work.

Now I Understand

"Now I understand you"—and especially with "see," we use the corollary "clear." My glasses the other day had a bunch of dust on them, more than usual, because we were out in the desert, and it wasn't clear anymore. Or maybe I made a mistake with this prescription. I thought I graduated out of bifocals and I hadn't. I thought, "Oh no, I am a youngster. I don't need bifocals." And now I always have these red marks on my forehead because I am always moving my glasses when looking down. It is not clear. I need my bifocals back for clarity's sake, please, and for my poor forehead. So that is a sight word that we also use for understanding. Clear. Sight. I see now, I understand. There is no way one could possibly turn this into a physical sight. Now I understand, and there is something to this. There is a personal side of this, too: I'd heard a report of this person; now I know them. That is the contrast with hearing and sight. And sight gives us more details of the world in one way than hearing does. And so, we say, I'd heard of you, but now I know you. And what work of God does Job know? It is not limited to saying, "Wow, God's really powerful and designs things." Job had said that earlier in the book. "Now I know the work of God in my life. I hadn't seen what is clear and God brought this to me, this redemptive work of God." None of those commentaries I mentioned come close to this. "Now I know it is clear God exists. This is my highest good. And it is clear in the works of Creation and Providence."

In Job 8:20, remember some of these things his friends said, which come back to them. Bildad said, "Surely God does not reject a blameless man or strengthen the hand of an evildoer." Bildad had also said, if you are good, you'll get good things; if you are bad, you will get bad things. But there is some truth to this. God did not reject Job, did he? He did not turn from Job. This is the loving discipline of God here. And we wonder this—it does not talk about the three friends, but it does say they came with Job. We wonder how much they grew in this with Job. Did they come to see this as well, that kind of detail, to say, "yeah, God doesn't reject us"? There is one way where we look at that suffering and say, "That guy's in hard times; God must hate him, but I was wrong about that." But there is another way in which God brings us through this suffering to greater understanding of him. Or we can take what Eliphaz said in 5:17: "Blessed is the man whom God corrects. So do not despise the discipline of the Almighty." It came in the context of telling Job he did things that he hadn't done, so Eliphaz was wrong. But what he said is still a truth, isn't it? Blessed is the man that God disciplines. That is all the way down into the New Testament.

Root Sin

So there is this repentance exemplified by Job, and some examples of this are, "I despise myself. And now I repent." Think of how this is said in, for example, Mark 1, where we have both John the Baptist and Jesus. Mark 1:4: "John came baptizing in the desert region and preaching a baptism of repentance for the forgiveness of sins." Repentance and baptism, forgiveness and cleansing. John came preaching those things. Repent, rethink, change your mind. You are wrong about these things. Or in Mark 15, after John was put in prison, Jesus went into Galilee proclaiming the good news of God. "'The time has come,' he said. 'The Kingdom of God is near. Repent and believe the good news'" (Mark 1:15). Repent about what? We know how the Pharisees struggled on this. Or the young man who said, "I have kept the law since my youth" (Matt 10:20). Maybe he thought of himself as blameless like Job. He should have read Job. Pay attention. Rethink it. You are not understanding. Or in Acts 2:37, while Peter is ending his speech, he says, "'Therefore, let all Israel be assured of this: God has made this Jesus, whom you crucified, both Lord and Christ.' When the people heard this, they were cut to the heart and said to Peter and to the other apostles, 'Brothers, what shall we do?' Peter replied, 'Repent and be baptized, every one of you, in the name of Jesus Christ, for the forgiveness of your sins.'" Repent. When we read these things from Mark or Acts we say, yeah, of course, that is New Testament stuff, Anderson. Here we have this book of Job, so early in human history, as the example of that.

Repent—of what? We did not see what was clear about God. And look at all that we humans have gone into. I saw a story where some archaeologists had made some advances understanding a temple outside Mexico City, where the priests would wear the human flesh of their sacrifices. We can see here how close and far they are. They are remembering a person must be covered by the death of another, and they are seeing that it cannot be an animal to represent a human. How badly they go into a mistake after that point. A human sacrifice, and this one must cover us. Remembering back to that promise but putting it into our own framework that denies the reality of root sin. We need to identify and repent of root sin. You should have seen what is clear about God.

Job came to this understanding only after the series of trials that we have now seen. There was no shortcut to it. Those are the details we must get into for our own lives. When we reflect on ourselves, what will it take to get us to think again and look into the details of God's work in our life? And maybe we haven't come to that point yet. The "conviction of sin and death" is the theological term. I am not saying that by way of suggesting a person is not a Christian if they did not put repentance in these terms. There are people one will meet who are quite older and they still say, "I don't remember ever having a time like that where I can pinpoint that." And it does not mean they did not; it means they need to think back and find it and see if they did. Or maybe they did not. They haven't ever been convicted of this root sin. We could be convicted of the pains that sins bring into our life or others' lives and learn our lesson from those. "Well, I'll never do that again. I'll never make that mistake again. I'll make different mistakes again." We can become very good at not making those kinds of mistakes and harming others, and yet we have never been convicted of sin and death for failing to see God. Those are different. As we go through Job, we have to ask that of ourselves as well. Have I seen this?

Sacrifice

God said to Eliphaz the Temanite, "I am angry with you and your two friends." Notice it is just those three that he is angry with, not Elihu. "Because you've not spoken what is right of me, as my servant Job has" (42:7). I want to pause there, because what is he talking about? God had also said Job spoke incorrectly—he is justifying himself. So in what way is Job saying some things that are the right thing about God when God just said he isn't? It can't just be a blanket statement—everything Job said is right. Specifically, here and now, Job is speaking the right things about God. Job is affirming, "I hadn't seen you as I should have."

Then God tells the friends to take seven bulls and seven rams and go to "his servant Job." This is God's servant Job from the very beginning. And we are not going to hear from Satan here, but he is present in our thinking about it, because we remember the heavenly realm. There was that original conflict, and Satan said, "Oh, Job only loves you for this reason?" Here we are, Job vindicated, he is God's servant. He came through this. He was the whole time. Go to him. Job works in the role of priest here for his friends, and the sacrifice is reminding them of their need for our sins to be covered by the death of another.

God says his servant Job will offer the sacrifice and will pray for them, and God will accept his prayer and not deal with them according to their folly. These three "wise men." Here is the pronouncement of God: their folly. They should have known these same things. "What you have spoken about me was not right." But what do they do? We get enough here in the text to know. They did what the Lord told them, and the Lord accepted Job's prayer. They, as well, come through this. The three friends come through—through Job's life example and now his ministry in offering the sacrifices. Job's friends come through this, and he forgives them. Would it take us a while to forgive them? "Where were you when I needed you?" Job forgives them because he knows he is forgiven.

Restoration and Fruit

Then the chapter says, "After Job had prayed for his friends, the Lord made him prosperous again and gave him twice as much as he had before" (42:10). Now we get a little bit of a picture, because we wonder how this happened, and I want to address this as we end, because I have heard the whole point of Job blunted by adding this on. "Oh, yeah, of course, he got everything back. Things went well for him." Someone may say, "In my case, I was suffering and I repented, and I am still suffering. So the book of Job is not helpful." I am going to say no; Job is helpful, whatever the case is. And if someone is going into it that way, they've already probably not repented in the sense that they are saying, "Yeah, I did not get stuff. I said sorry, but no stuff showed up. I said sorry but I am still having health problems. So I guess God's not upholding me." Now they are back to the middle of the book, right? They are not doing at all what Job did. So why does the story end up this way here?

Another way people blunt the story is by saying it is kind of a Hallmark ending. And I wondered at the beginning if people's favorite movie might be a Hallmark one. Oh, yes, they always have the perfect rhythm of conflict and resolution, and then usually a wedding at the end—it is just wonderful. Everyone ends up happy. So, we put the movie on 24/7 and we will just be happy because we see these happy endings. It is a shadow of the Shakespearean comedies, and the Shakespearean comedies themselves are representations of Christian history. All things end up in the wedding supper of the Lamb.

So why do things end up like that? I have heard Job put bluntly, saying, "Yeah, that is great for Job, but it does not work out that way for me." What are the details of that? In 42:11, it tells us some details: "All his brothers and sisters and everyone who had known him before came and ate with him at his house. They comforted and consoled him over all the trouble the Lord had brought upon him. And each one of them gave him a piece of silver and a gold ring (Job 42:11)." It is an interesting contrast between the earlier comforters and these comforters. After his repentance, coming through in his understanding, his restoration begins with them giving him these gifts. Those gifts aren't all of the restoration, but that is the beginning of it. They give these offerings to help him. And it is interesting; it says, "The trouble the Lord had brought upon him." How would Job have heard that statement at the beginning, and how does he hear it now? That is a large part of the question we have: is it worth it? Is the suffering worth the spiritual growth/repentance from root sin? "I am okay with losing my camels; but boils—I am not okay with that." We might try to negotiate something with God. When is it worth it? Here that phrase is used; earlier Job had asked, why is God troubling me? Now he knows. So, when we ask the question it will affect the answer.

We should know in the beginning and middle, not just the end, what God is doing. God has been disciplining Job. We are going to look at a few verses about that. Proverbs 3:12: "For whom the Lord loves he corrects, just as a father the son in whom he delights." That is Proverbs. Because then we'll get into Hebrews 12:6, and it sounds like the same thing—it is like Paul read Solomon. "Because the Lord disciplines the one he loves and he chastens everyone he accepts as a son." And we know that we are to count it all joy when we go through trials of many kinds for these reasons (James 1:2). We get that picture of the loving hand of God in discipline in both the Old Testament and the New Testament. And we have the example of Job. Before we really get into any more special revelation, we need to know this. We did not reckon with the problem of evil before we got into the rest of special revelation. This is the problem of understanding original sin, the first sin. What is sin? And what is the role, therefore, of natural evil that comes out on us because of that? In that way this book is a prolegomenon. And if Moses wrote Job, we can reflect on how he understood it in relation to the Pentateuch.

Then we get the restoration of Job's things. This section mentions the sheep, camels, oxen, donkeys—and children. And especially it mentions the names of his daughters. They were given an inheritance along with their brothers. We might wonder this: Job gets a double of everything else; why not a double of children? Was there not enough time? He could have twins each time. If it is double of everything he could have twins every time. Well, in contrast to the animals or the wealth, the first children are not gone. He does have the double. They are still in existence and they will still be restored at the resurrection. So, we have Job restored back to where he was. And this conclusion: "After this, Job lived 140 years. He saw his children and their children to the fourth generation. And so he died, old and full of years."

Was all of this worth it? Well, it depends what the "it" is. Was all of this worth coming to a greater knowledge of God? It probably depends when you ask

Job that question. In the middle of the trial he may very well say "no." But at the end he acknowledges a greater knowledge of God and repentance, meaning that he should have done this before. He does this instead of complaining.

Was all of this suffering necessary? That is different from "is it worth it," because it could be worth it but done in an easier way. The necessity is related to the hardness of the heart. Throughout this text I have asked what will it take for us to see our root sin. Natural evil is the answer. An objection along the lines of Ivan Karamazov is that the innocent suffering is not fair or justified. I think specifically of Job's children. They had to suffer and die in order for Job to come to learn more.

We are often struck by the death of a child more than by the death of an adult. But the problem is the same: why is there death at all? Why does anybody have to die? Physical death was not original. It was imposed after moral evil. And as moral evil is removed so too will be physical death. So rather than being occupied by physical death, which already says there is a problem in our thinking, we should be occupied by the depth of moral evil. Ivan will say that the children are innocent so they have not yet committed certain outward sins. Physical death is not the end, as we have an immortal soul. Additionally, physical death is not a punishment for our sins. The innocence of a child with respect to those sins is not sufficient to raise a problem about why they have physical death. Presumably, after death, one will continue to think and the reality of death will continue to serve as a callback to think about basic things. Whether or not one will think about basic things is another question. Physical death is the last call back. If a person did not heed that final call back, then they will not hear any other additional calls back.

Job is aware that his children might be sinning and offered sacrifices for them. Perhaps the idea is that if only someone had more time then they might have come to know God. But the sovereignty of God has been central to this whole account. A person comes out in a relationship to God exactly where God wants them to. More time won't change that, and less time can't interrupt that. A person needs a new heart, regeneration, which is an act of God, not an act of human will or time plus opportunity. Job's children were not merely a means to something for Job, they have their own stories and their own root sin that they need to deal with.

Death is unnatural. It is one of the reasons we have the struggle over the problem of evil. It is unnatural at any age. This is a problem not just for children but for humans. We should not allow the idea that children are innocent of some kinds of sins to distract us from the fact of death itself, and the need to give an account. Why was death imposed on humanity at all? Dying of old age is not somehow better and more acceptable compared to dying from sickness or famine or war. They are all death. And wrestling with the horror of death invites wrestling with the horror of sin. And only wrestling with fruit sins won't be sufficient. Even though they can be heinous, these fruit sins don't explain why the world is filled with misery. We need to wrestle with root sin and our condition before God.

There is a similar phrase used later of Abraham: a full life. What counts as a full life? Seeing your children to that generation. But don't turn that simply into numbers. "I saw so many kids and so many generations." We already know from the beginning of the book Job's concern for his children, offering sacrifices for them. He is seeing the fruit to the third and fourth generation. That is what brought Job contentment and a full life. We can look at how Aristotle wrestles with how to know we have lived a good life, or how Cicero and Cato debate about this. They are all wrong. They all deny what is clear about God from the works of God and so fall completely short of knowing what is a full life. If someone told me Job had a full life because he had the animals and money back, I would say they badly missed it. That is why those last verses of 42, 16 and

17, connect to that, the fullness of life, with seeing those generations. Bearing fruit and fruit that will last. That is what Job had. And that is available to anybody, because someone could say, "Oh, I did not get my stuff back like I said earlier; I did not get my health back or whatever it was in my particular trial." Nothing would prevent someone from being fruitful, bearing fruit and leading a full life in that.

Application

Think about the application of it to the Church today. The application to our own life today. Christians say they have repented of sin. Do they say they have repented of root sin? This does not mean that they use that terminology. But do they repent of not having seen what is clear about God in general revelation? This is repentance of root sin. And it includes turning from this sin to now seek to know what is clear about God from general revelation. This is what Job did. But look at what it took to get him to that place.

Have we had the experience of Job? And if we say, "Well, if that is what it takes to be a Christian, I prefer not"...Well, it won't have all those details, but it will be unique in our own life. People like to share their stories of suffering. "Let me tell you how hard my life is." It is way harder, by implication, than yours. People like to have a suffering competition. We have all suffered. Have we made sense of it? Have we come to the conviction that we came short of the glory of God in a blameworthy way, to say we abhor ourselves? Does that sound too strong to our ears? I abhor myself for coming short of the glory of God. Look how that gets so beautifully to root sin in Job. Not that I abhor myself for these other things that we usually put up there. "I abhor myself for my fruit sin" is not getting to root sin. I abhor myself because now I see You and I should have seen You before. Now I see God why didn't I before? This is conviction of sin and death. And that is why we had this at the very beginning of history. It serves as a solution, for those who have eyes to see, of the great problem facing humans.

There is no doubt that the Church is currently divided. Badly divided. The world sees this division. There are calls for the Church to make changes. To confess sin. If there are to be changes then what needs to be confessed first is root sin. This is also where the divisions can find unity. This gets us back to the most foundational truths on which the rest of the edifice is built. Repent, for the kingdom of God is at hand.

Conviction of root sin. The conviction of the failure to see what is clear about God and turning from that as sin. We might try to get conviction some other way without going through that, trying to get around it. That is like getting back into the garden without justification and sanctification. So, we need to use this to come to see ourselves the way Job saw himself: God and man. Basic things. Coming to see ourselves as inexcusable for sin. Not just the principle of sin and death, but the conviction of sin and death. And that conviction working in the context of the curse and the promise: the curse calling us back to see this in terms of our moral evil, our root sin of not seeking God and seeing what is clear about God in all the works of God.

What About Satan?

Concluding with the scene in heaven: a point was being made there. We saw Satan come and challenge God and Job, but we know that God had brought up Job: "Have you considered my servant Job?" And this is a servant that we are to consider as well, from the beginning down to the present. God is revealing this, not only to other human beings on earth, post-Job (the answers were there before Job), but also to the principalities and the powers and the heavenly realm, showing the manifold wisdom of God. Satan did not get the outcome that he wanted. Job did not curse God to his face, but it also wasn't that he merely held on—"I won't curse God, I won't curse God, I won't curse God." Rather, he broke through to a new level of understanding. He wasn't merely adding information. No: I was convicted at a deeper level. This tells us about the spiritual battle. Talk about slaying a dragon. This is the battle between good and evil, between belief and unbelief. We can think of Romans 8:18: "I consider our present sufferings are not worth comparing with the glory that will be revealed in us." Satan was not mentioned at the end, and he does not need to be. His folly was exposed for all to see. That is also part of the revelation. The attempt backfired. Not only did Job not curse God to his face; Job saw the redemptive work of God and said "Now I see you." Job moved, he grew, he praised the glorious work of God.

The Glory of God

Have we come to see more about the glory that was revealed in Job? This is given by God and meant to be meditated upon. Consider my servant Job—over and over—consider my servant Job. And with Job, I was reminded of Psalm 145:5 and 7: Job directs us not simply to consider himself, but to consider the works of God. Psalm 145: "Upon Thy glorious majesty and wondrous works, my mind shall dwell. Men shall recount Thy dreadful acts, and of Thy greatness I will tell. They utter shall abundantly the memory of Thy goodness great, and shall sing praises cheerfully, while they Thy righteousness relate." We take from this not just what Job went through, but directing ourselves to God and the dreadful, mighty acts of God. We see the mightiness of God's working with Job and each one of us, and recounting those works. We can tell the nations of the story of Job and the work of God. The nations learn the fear of the Lord. This story can bring us to be able to say, "Now my eyes see you." And that is what it means to consider God's servant Job.

Bibliography

Andersen, Francis. Job (Tyndall Old Testament Commentaries Book 14). IVP Academic, 2015.

Ash, Christopher. Job: The Wisdom of the Cross. Crossway, 2014.

Belcher, Richard. Job: The Mystery of Suffering and God's Sovereignty. Christian Focus, 2017.

Brown, Michael. Job: The Faith to Challenge God: A New Translation and Commentary. Henrdickson, 2019.

Calvin, John. Sermons on Job. Reformation Heritage Books.

Caryl, Joseph. Practical Observations on Job, 12 Vols. Reformation Heritage Books. (Original 1644-1666).

Ellison, H.L. A Study of Job: From Tragedy to Triumph. Zondervan, 1974.

Fyall, Robert. Now My Eyes Have Seen You: Images of Creation and Evil in the Book of Job (New Studies in Biblical Theology). IVP Academic, 2002.

Greenstein, Edward L. Job: A New Translation. Yale University Press, 2019.

Hartley, John E. The Book of Job (The New International Commentary on the Old Testament). Eerdmans, 1988.

Havel, Norman C. The Book of Job: A Commentary (The Old Testament Library). Westminster John Knox Press, 1985.

Henry, Matthew. Matthew Henry's Commentary One Volume. Zondervan Academic, 1961.

Jung, C. G. Answer to Job. Princeton University Press, 2010.

Kidner, Derek. The Wisdom of Proverbs, Job & Ecclesiastes. IVP Academic, 2015.

Simonetti, Manlio. Job (Ancient Christian Commentary on Scripture). IVP Academic, 2006.

Williams, C.J. The Shadow of Christ in the Book of Job. Wipf and Stock, 2017.

Index

J

K

M

N

O

P

R

S

U

W

CPSIA information can be obtained
at www.ICGtesting.com
Printed in the USA
BVHW051047070421
604337BV00029B/3218/J